BUDDHISM
for Beginners

The Step-by-Step Guide to Overcome the Era of Anxiety and Stress Using Mindfulness Meditation and Zen Teachings

Sarah Allen

© Copyright 2020 by Sarah Allen - All rights reserved

This document is geared towards providing exact and reliable information about the topic and issue covered. The publication is sold with the idea that the publisher is not required to render accounting, officially permitted, or otherwise qualified services. If advice is necessary, legal, or professional, a practiced individual in the profession should be ordered.

From a Declaration of Principles which was accepted and approved equally by a Committee of the American Bar Association and a Committee of Publishers and Associations.

In no way is it legal to reproduce, duplicate, or transmit any part of this document in either electronic means or printed format. Recording of this publication is strictly prohibited, and any storage of this document is not allowed unless with written permission from the publisher. All rights reserved.

The information provided herein is stated to be truthful and consistent, in that any liability, in terms of inattention or otherwise, by any usage or abuse of any policies, processes, or directions contained within is the solitary and utter responsibility of the recipient reader. Under no circumstances will any legal responsibility or blame be held against the publisher for any reparation, damages, or monetary loss due to the information herein, either directly or indirectly.

Respective authors own all copyrights not held by the publisher.

The information herein is offered for informational purposes solely and is universal as so.

The presentation of the information is without a contract or any guarantee assurance.

The trademarks that are used are without any consent, and the publication of the trademark is without permission or backing by the trademark owner. All trademarks and brands within this book are for clarifying purposes only and are owned by the owners themselves, not affiliated with this document.

TABLE OF CONTENTS

INTRODUCTION 9
CHAPTER 1 13
  Knowing Your Mind 13
  Fixed Mindset Vs Growth Mindset 19
  Growth Mindset 23
  Best Strategies to Find Your Balance and
  Inner Peace 28
  Anger Management 41
  Don't Let Fear Control Your Life........................... 47
  How to Overcome Serious Hardship &
  Adversity 53
  Best Strategies To Healing Yourself 64
CHAPTER 2 84
  What is Buddhism?... 84
  Origins of Buddhism 84
  The Story of Siddhārtha Gautama....................... 86
  Buddhism 101... 88
  The Basics of Buddhism... 89
  5 Steps to Start Buddhist Meditation 92
  A Typical Day 100
CHAPTER 3.. 105
  The Teaching of Buddhism................................. 105
  The Noble Eightfold Path 106
  Dharma - The Path to Perfect Enlightenment ... 108
  Suffering and Neurosis 109

- What Is Non-Self? 110
- What Are the Sutras? 110
- What Is Karma? 111
- What Is Reincarnation? 113
- What Is the Abhidharma? 114
- What Is Yoga? 114
- Postures of Buddha 115
- 5 Zen Buddhism Teachings 116

CHAPTER 4 118
- Buddhism Numbers 3 118
- The 3 Jewels of Refuge 118
- The 3 Higher Trainings 118
- The 3 Universal Truths 121
- The 3 Poisons 124
- The Different Schools of Buddhism 125
- Mahayana 125
- Vajrayana 126
- Buddhist Philosophy 101 126
- The 4 Noble Truths 127
- The 4 Dharma Seals 128
- The 5 Skandhas 129
- The 5 Precepts of Buddhism 129
- Perfections of Buddhism 130
- The 6 Perfections of Mahayana Buddhism 131

CHAPTER 5 132
- Mindfulness Meditation 132
- Benefits of Mindfulness 133

- Training the Mind 134
- Freeing your Mind 135
- Classic Mindfulness Meditation Step-By-Step ... 135
- Repeat the process until your meditation sessions end. 137
- Different Buddhist Rituals 137
- CHAPTER 6 138
- Japanese Buddhism 138
- Buddhism In This Era 138
- Creating a Meditation Space in Your Home 141
- 5 Steps to Start Buddhist Meditation 142
- How to Practice Buddhism 142
- Practicing Mindfulness Meditation for Stress and Anxiety Relief 144
- Buddhism for Children 147
- CHAPTER 7 151
- CONCLUSION 151

INTRODUCTION

The creation and control of the universe are unarguably from a higher source. This is a phenomenon that human beings have tried to understand over the years. Connecting with a supreme being and efforts to get connected to that source have made man experience forces beyond compare. There are various degrees of participation in the quest to discover the inner self that connects to a deity. This has been the hallmark of the factors that seem to unite all human beings in the world. Although not everybody believes in anything that has to do with the supernatural, someplace their beliefs in other philosophies. Science-based beliefs don't dwell on anything that cannot be proven scientifically. Of course, there has always been disagreement over the years on what should be believed or what ought not to be believed, what exists or what doesn't exist, or what can be seen or what cannot be seen. The spirituality of man and his embodiment in the physical has been interpreted by some people with beliefs in the supernatural to have a divine connection with a superior being. And this leads us to what we now know in the world as religion.

We have various religions in the world, and there is a diversity that comes with people who place their beliefs in different things, both living and non-living. Despite that, there is one particular religion that is exceptional and based purely on practical terms, on what can be practiced, and the result is seen accordingly. This religion does not force you to believe, but it makes you see reality. It is convincing enough for you to admit the facts because they appear just as they are. Many people in the world are yet to discover themselves or know who they really are. The practice of Buddhism is quite different and exceptional in the sense that it is all-encompassing and consuming. It teaches the individual to identify himself with the possibility of physical and spiritual advancement. This will re-orientate him to have a different conception about life and see it from a more spiritual angle. This, with great authority, will show what is obtainable from the natural through spiritual concentration and communication with a higher source of power. Inevitably, it results in a practical approach to recognizing and communicating with the mind.

A Buddhist student will be transformed and given the necessary training and wisdom that comes with transformation. He becomes a new being capable of identifying and touching lives in magnificent and influential ways. The teachings, based on practical knowledge, evolve the way to self-actualization. New knowledge transformation can also be traced and noticed in the individual's way of thinking and expression whenever the need arises. The Buddhist student becomes the epitome of knowledge of what an individual is capable of becoming, achieved within the space and time of practicing the knowledge imparted through Buddhism. The beginners who learn the art of Buddhism as a religion and practice it faithfully will become exceptionally outstanding among their peers. They will command authority with a different mindset and way of thinking that exceeds the ordinary citizen. In addition, Buddhists are masters whenever they make commentaries about life and how it should be lived.

While many religions successfully command followers, the Buddhist faith has successfully created more potential leaders because of its knowledge impartation. This actually goes with the practice that leads to the transformation of individuals. No matter their status, they are able to learn the actual meaning and truth about life, as well as how it should be lived. Self-examination, combined with a high level of spirituality, is very effective in Buddhism practice. This is one of the keys that guarantee great success when anyone applies the Buddhist system of belief and practice. When a student of Buddhism gets involved in the real practice of the Buddhist faith, this is the turning point in the life of such an individual. Many Buddhists are known all over the world to have the most effective and exceptional lifestyles. Almost all other religions can borrow a leaf from the way of life of the Buddhist.

There is an enormous misconception about the term "Buddhism," especially from the Western part of the world. Buddhism has a deeply traditional and practical orientation. It is further believed to work perfectly in modern times. This is because it can be applied in the modern lifestyle to solve the problems of anxiety and stress through improved mindfulness mediation. Also, this is achieved by following the Zen pathway. Enjoy!

CHAPTER 1

Knowing Your Mind

How well do you know yourself? Before you can answer this question, you have to understand your mind. The mind leads to the success and failures of many people, but for a person who practices Buddhism, it helps the development of his mind. What causes the difference in many people around the world starts from the mind. It is based on mindsets that we can distinguish great people from people who are going to fail in their course. Every individual has a mindset level. Your mindset level of understanding or positivity can differ from another person's. This is why we will never stop having individuals with different mindsets. As long as we are different human beings, we are bound to have different mindsets. Now I will be taking you through the Buddhist system of mindset. Also, how it all begins and ends with the level of perception of the individual, which is responsible for the success and advancement of his destiny and which can impact greatly on him.

The mind is powerful in the sense that it determines who you are. The fact that you are resolute and wouldn't want to change your mind doesn't make you an exceptional individual. Rather, an exceptional individual is one who is able to adapt, adjust, and become more flexible to understandings and teachings. The mind is very powerful because it goes a long way to define a person's stance on issues. It also defines an individual's perception of life and how it can turn around to affect him personally, throughout his life. How well you discover your mindset and levels of seeing through the mind is something that is not easy to accomplish. Especially without some form of education and teaching that will help you to open up your mind. While a closed mind is a closed destiny, a lot has to do with an individual's acceptability and readiness to assume the position of a victor by being open. I say this because not many people are prepared to allow the impact of knowledge and teachings that can transform them.

Therefore, can you force knowledge on someone? It depends; if the age of knowledge is necessary, then yes, of course. But for an adult, it may not be easy—you cannot change him because he is already adamant. Most people have such problems. Opening up the mind to allow knowledge and training that will be very useful can be difficult for some people. However, this is not to say that we cannot have the knowledge imparted; it just requires discipline. If such individuals can be disciplined enough to listen, then the knowledge can strike them below the belt, and they will stay humble and listen.

The individual may be going through a lot of difficulties during the knowledge impartation. This is usually the case where the mind is not stable. So it's always advisable to allow such a person to get a stable mindset before the knowledge can sink into the brain. Because knowledge impartation is continued, it will be a waste of time, effort, and resources. A lot of people are distracted in life, which gives them a low level of mindset control. Furthermore, the ability to stay focused is always a problem. They keep thinking of the problems that are bothering them. Buddhism will help you in such circumstances because you will learn how to remain focused. The level of mental concentration in Buddhism is higher compared to any form of religion because the people who do more concentration of the mind through hours of meditation are Buddhists.

There is no way you can defeat a Buddhist who knows his mind because he has a much higher level of mental concentration. He practices more mind development and advancement, enabling him to communicate with a higher source, discover himself the more, and have better enlightenment. How well you know your mind is very important because you meet people on a daily basis and communicate. This leads to the interrelationship between people; their reaction and responses toward you may or may not affect you. And this depends on if you have a mind that can take anything, no matter how bad it is. The question now is, how strong is your mind to receive unfavorable remarks or comments that can be regarded as derogatory? This is one important area where Buddhism will help you.

Another aspect I will be talking about knowing your mind is your mindset during the competition, when you compete with others in games, at offices, business, or school. In these environments, there is usually some level of competition. The question is, how prepared is your mind to go through such competition and also win? Even if you win, how would you manage the situation when people try to bring you down? In such circumstances, you will need to know if your mindset can take criticism or attacks akin to those experienced by champions. Do you have the mind of a champion? That is the big question; hence, practicing Buddhism will help you handle such challenges. You don't need to leave your country to visit India or Asia to practice Buddhism. No, you can do this by simply following the laid down pragmatic knowledge as presented in this book.

Again, your mind is who you are. So if you are very timid and fearful, whether you like it or not, people will soon know that you are hiding who you really are and that you have a fearful mind. This can change if you are able to practice Buddhism because it helps to develop your mind. There is always a need to practice Buddhism because of situations that will require you to have a strong mind. Your mindset will determine if you will be able to handle difficult situations. If you have found yourself in a very difficult situation, knowing the kind of mindset that you have will enable you to determine if you will overcome it or not. Most people in the world today are unable to face difficult situations and often unable to overcome the situations they find themselves in. You can actually get things done or defeat the situation you find yourself in if it is really difficult as a Buddhist, and you learn to have a strong mind. But if you are unable to develop a strong mind, you will find it difficult to beat such situations. The truth is, many people in the world today are affected by adverse situations. They seem unable to deal with it, and that's why they are what they are because of the mindset they have.

If you are poor, you may have been born that way, but that doesn't mean you should remain poor. No, if you have the right mind, you can advance and free yourself from that situation. This will happen if you have the mindset of a successful person. You can become rich with self-determination to make money, and that will only happen if you have a mind that can carry you through the process of becoming rich. Becoming rich may not come easy, but it is really possible if you are able to learn the power of knowing your mind and developing it.

In the political circle, we have leaders who have spent some years preparing for leadership, while others never really took time to prepare for it. Great leaders like Mahatma Gandhi of India, prepared for leadership. As a leader, he spent years studying and practicing the art of knowing the mind to fight a just cause, which was void of using weapons. All over the world, he remains one of the most talked-about leaders from Asia with a great gift of mind control and human leadership qualities that can change a course of action. Meanwhile, there are other leaders who think that power involves owning a weapon and using it to intimidate others or wage war and win. How wrong they are. If only they could see that they are just weak people with weak minds that cannot influence anyone in their course. They are only able to do this with the barrel of a gun or a weapon.

Preparing yourself for the future also means you have to prepare your mind for the tasks ahead. You can only do that by understanding your mindset. If you don't know your mind, then you cannot start to achieve anything. You will only exist as a normal human being who doesn't know anything other than the fact that he is just like any other person. Understanding and knowing your mind will also help you to connect with your partner, the person who is right for you. Both of you will be able to know and understand each other. This will make you a perfect match for each other when you are in a relationship or seeking to find a life partner. Knowing how being intimate with your partner will lead to bonding is a necessary factor in marriage. It is not just loving a person alone that matters, but when the connection is there, there will be a complete bonding. This cannot take place without knowing the kind of minds that you and your partner have.

Fixed Mindset Vs Growth Mindset

A fixed mindset, as the name implies, means that you are unable to develop your mindset or change it from the present state because of your personality type. You find it difficult to change your mindset, and that is bound to affect you in everything that you do. A fixed mindset remains adamant and unwilling to change. This can be linked to real-life circumstances where we have people who are unable to accept things the way they are or are unyielding because they just don't want to change their mindset about something. One of the major reasons people do not make progress in whatever they do is because they have a fixed mindset. They are unable and unwilling to shift their mind towards something different from what they are used to.

There are several factors that are associated with a fixed mindset. It is very important to learn and know when to have a fixed mindset, and when not to have it. Not that a fixed mindset cannot be applied in some circumstances, but it should be understood that a fixed mindset as defined is totally different for a person who has it and can adapt to the use of it.

A fixed mindset can be shifted when the need arises. When the position of a belief system comes to play, one can fix his mind on what he believes in. For example, if you believe in yourself and that you will be successful, that kind of mindset is acceptable because you fixed it on something that has to do with your belief system. It's something that you fixed your mind about yourself. You believe in yourself; it's about you, it's going to work, and you don't doubt yourself. In this case, that becomes a positively fixed mindset. But when you refuse to have a change of mindset, are unwilling to learn, and remain adamant in the face of opportunities that can change your life for the better, then that becomes a negatively fixed mindset. And this is very unhealthy. The reason why several people are poor today is because they have a negatively fixed mindset. One that is unwilling to accept the change or opportunity, and that is why they remain where they are in life.

A fixed mindset, therefore, has different meanings in different circumstances. The more you are able to understand this, the more likely you will become in tune with the practice of Buddhism. The power of the mind cannot be overemphasized. Fixing your mindset on something is what makes you think of it, and place your focus on that thing. Fixing your mindset on something that you know will happen leads to expectation. Expectations can come out positive or negative, depending on what is involved—understanding matters when it comes to the practice of Buddhism. The right mindfulness and understanding in the practice of Buddhism is really important because the practice is based on the mind of the individual, coupled with the ability to understand and read meanings to events and situations of life.

A fixed mindset can be healthy, but it can also be unhealthy. Buddhism teaches happiness and inner spirituality that lead to self-discovery, as well as fixing your mind positively on gaining happiness. Happiness can be obtained through self-suffering. Now, liberating yourself from worldly attachments opens up your mind to become a new human being through rebirth to a new self, leaving your old self to the memories of the past but still remaining fresh. This is a positive way of fixing your mindset on something that is acceptable and practicable.

An unhealthy mindset makes an individual reject the right way of doing things. Always reacting instead of responding to situations based on the conscience of the mind is very different and can constitute a negatively fixed mindset. The individual with a negatively fixed mindset is always a problem in the society. This is because he is always thinking adversely against the acceptable standards, especially when contemporary society is involved. A negatively fixed mindset individual may not bring peace; he may not be open to dialogue and is more aggressive than others. This is the major problem of conflict that we have in the world today.

Many individuals who engage in violence always have these problems, such as the terrorist who has a fixed mindset on carrying out acts of terrorism. These kinds of people have already fixed their minds on such negativity and are not ready to change it. They would rather die as terrorists than convert to responsible human beings. This is not about religion alone, but it's also about the individual's disposition and nature of how he views and accepts the society. As well as how he wants to enforce his beliefs on people and control the society based on his own standards. Fixed mindset individuals don't believe that other peoples' opinions count, and they would do whatever it takes to enforce their beliefs on people. Such a mindset is very unhealthy and is simply fixated on negativity.

A fixed mindset, if wrongfully applied, doesn't guarantee progress in the life of an individual. Mindfulness is a very essential and helpful part of the practice of Buddhism. An aspirant about to enter into the terrain of mind practice and spirituality of one of the largest, most well-recognized religions in the world and one of the renowned religions that have to do with mindfulness and consciousness of self-growth, should be prepared to shoulder a responsible way of life.

Growth Mindset

Despite the fact that the fixed mindset person has difficulty changing as a result of fixing his mind on what is not rewarding or positive, there can always be a shift in his fixated mindset. There can always be a way out, a mindset growth, which comes in different phases. It can be a process of re-birth and rehabilitation. The re-birth process is always associated with Buddhism, while rehabilitation has to do with individuals who have been submerged in circumstances that have gone deep into their minds. Rehabilitation is usually for people with the following problems; drinking, drug-related problems, alcoholism, and insanity, etc. These are some circumstances that influence people through used substances or depression. There is a variance in what it takes for mind growth and rehabilitation. Rehabilitation processes are always handled by professionals. They have been trained and educated extensively in an institution of higher learning in methods of taking care of those with troubled minds such as those mentioned above.

But when it comes to the growth of the mind in Buddhism, we are consciously involved in the development of the mind. This is achieved through set down pragmatic practice that makes use of purely natural processes such as meditation, concentration, self-discovery, and spirituality. The practice of Buddhism is wholesomely to achieve the form of re-birth that changes the individual's conception and orientation to a new human being void of negativity.

The spiritual level of success is a unique way of spiritual growth, which is always associated with the practice. This is coupled with the help of the belief system that connects to a higher source and that the individuals have an inner self-conscious path in life.

Growth of the mind is when your mind gradually develops into a unique state that enables you to see things through it. You come across a problem. You are able to identify it and take measures that can bring about a lasting solution. The development of the mind doesn't stop with you; it radiates and touches lives. Through your mindfulness and understanding, you are able to create solutions that influence people who seem to be lost in problems that overwhelm them. You are special and different from others through the knowledge of the fact that you have a developed mind. You are able to pursue a course and achieve it easily. Buddhism teaches the mind growth phenomena, and this makes it possible for people to see and know the difference between the growth of the mind and a fixed mindset that doesn't yield to any teaching.

The growth of the mind is an essential feature of the teachings of Buddhism because the practice of Buddhism revolves around mind consciousness and development. When considering the factors of

Buddhism like meditation, the belief system, the teachings, the re-birth, re-examination, etc., you cannot help but believe in the fact that all these activities help in the advancement of the mind. And this actually brings a permanent mind growth. Many people around the world today are having problems with mental growth. Yes, you might say that education is the key to an individual's development. I agree with you, but at the same time, what is education to a mind that is not ready to accept it? Not everyone who went to school actually completed the education process because they were never prepared to accept education in the first place.

Secondly, many people who went to school started it from the cradle where it is easier to impart knowledge. It's almost certain that a child who is put through school doesn't have a choice than to embrace it. Of course, as the child grows and is developing, his will later settles into what he was meant or made to study. That is the knowledge he or she will have until such an individual decides to learn new things.

However, the Buddhist system creates awareness into a whole new level and dimension. It is practically based on self-determination and awareness that enhances an individual's development, irrespective of the level of education. The educated person, for instance, may not yet discover a link between a deeper understanding of himself with a conscious mind and another individual outside his environment. This is where the Buddhist is at an advantage. The Buddhist understands what true happiness and self-conviction really mean. He works hard to attain a higher level of mindfulness even if he has to go through some restrictions in life. He is always prepared to afflict himself with a great deal of discipline to get greater abilities through self-consciousness in Buddhism.

Learning Buddhism as a beginner means you have to free or liberate yourself from every distraction and make your mind available for the training. Having a good listening and learning attitude will help you have a deeper meaning of what Buddhism has to offer. Without this, you will not succeed. It is when you learn to listen to your inner self that you will become more successful. You have to make sure you attain a higher level of mindfulness by paying attention and feeling. Also, having the willingness to learn new ways of life such that after your conscious learning, you will become physically and spiritually advanced in your mode of understanding. Growth, therefore, will help you go a long way to measure the level of success. However, you need to understand and acquire the ability to listen and learn. Silence is important because you need to stay calm and learn the new re-birth and cleansing that you are actually subjecting yourself to attain during the process.

With a high level of mindfulness, which leads to openness to learning, be rest assured that your re-birth is something that will easily be noticed. It will reflect on virtually all the activities that you do. By the time you become regular in Buddhism, you will attain more heights. You will be able to realize the differences and misconceptions that other religions or belief systems have of Buddhism. That will be something great because you actually practice it, and it changes your life for the better. This will definitely reflect in the teaching and lifestyle that you will be born into.

Best Strategies to Find Your Balance and Inner Peace

Finding inner peace that gives you a total transformation to a new human being is very difficult in a world filled with deceit, untrustworthiness, jealousy, and insincerity. That's what many people go through on a daily basis. Many do not have an inner peace that makes them comfortable and smile in every situation. They are always having problems either with themselves or their neighbor. This is so because there is always an inner-self battle with the outside world, and many have to realize that the problem is actually not from the outside but from the inside. To be able to win the battle, you have to start from the inside to get the innermost insight that transcends more than what is on the outside. The belief system has a little part to play when you believe you can change from the inside to the outside. For instance, if a person doesn't accept you, it doesn't necessarily mean that they are right. Just because they don't accept you, doesn't mean you cannot be accepted by someone else.

There are people who are looking for you, and they need you more than others, it is left for you to make yourself available. Your availability will only come from your innermost conviction and not from the acceptability of others or what others think about you. It is so sad to see how people are becoming discouraged by the disapproval of others or the bad remarks they receive from others about them. Life doesn't teach us that everybody should speak well of us. Even the most outstanding of the prophets never got excellent comments from everyone.

To find inner peace, you must first discover yourself. Discovering yourself in a difficult world that is filled with grudges and unloving people does not change who you are. You are the one who can create the influential nature that is in you and which gives you happiness. Take a look at a person who is not happy. It is obvious when the person is not smiling, and you ask him, "My friend, what is the problem?" Then he replies, "I am not happy because something terrible just happened to me." Within you, you can feel the pain that he is going through because he is having a bad experience. But the question is, what can you do to help him out of that situation if you don't have inner peace yourself? This is why it is necessary to have inner peace before you can help other people get out of their situation. The first thing to note here is how to get inner peace for yourself.

Another discussion is "getting the balance in the inner peace that you have now." Some people think that when there is no war or conflict, there is peace. That is not true; the fact that there is no war doesn't mean that there is peace in a country or among nations. I remember a certain time in the 60s and 70s when there was no threat of war, but in actual fact, there was a different type of war that was going on the "Cold War." The Cold War era was about space dominance, and space technological development. Nations that were unable to explore space or the galaxy became afraid that someday, the western countries will get into space and dominate. And perhaps get better technology that can make them dominate any kind of warfare. Now that was one form of war that was not fought by the barrel of the gun, and it is still the same today, it hasn't changed.

We have seen nations talking about nuclear weapons. There is suspicion about developing nuclear weapons capable of wiping out an entire human race, and this is not a peaceful situation at all. There has to be an agreement, and everybody has to be on the same page. Everybody has to be at peace with one another; no one should be left out in the circumstances. The same goes for an individual. Your entire body must agree to have inner peace. You must be healthy in all parts of your body, not having pain in some parts. If you have pain in some parts, you cannot be peaceful in such circumstances because you will be distracted, thinking about that pain and how you can stop it.

The Buddhist student masters this and understands the entire discussion on finding the best strategies to get the inner balance of peace. The example mentioned earlier is related to how the man who got involved in Buddhism started. He also had a similar experience where there was a lot of tension in his environment. It was as if everybody was against each other. So much anger, misunderstanding, grief, complaining, pain, and people being unhappy and selfish. He wanted something that could give him inner peace since he wasn't finding it among people who were around him. This is the same scenario that an individual living in modern society always faces. There will always be confrontations and challenges coming from people around you. In the face of all these troubles, how will you be able to cope? What are the strategies you need to apply to free yourself from the numerous troubles that accompany this kind of person? Here I will explain some things that you need to do as an individual so you can free yourself from the shackles of backwardness.

Self-conviction is one of the most important things here: You have to be convinced that it is possible to achieve inner peace and balance with the strategy you are going to adopt. Conviction is the self-consciousness, perception, and acceptability that you are definitely on top of the situation. Never believe in what people say or think about you, having the mind that you can always have inner peace, and it doesn't have to come from someone else. Self-conviction is one of the major keys to attaining inner peace because you already know that your peace is within you, and it doesn't have to come from the outside. Despite what you are going through, your inner peace should remain intact. Once you know this, you will be able to create a balance between yourself and the inner peace consciousness. I never doubt myself once whenever it comes to creating a balance between my inner peace and what goes on around me.

I know circumstances will always come to take or draw that inner peace away from me, but I always remain resolute in the face of problems. Why? Because my inner peace is well-balanced. I am the one who has it and not someone else. It doesn't depend on others. Therefore, it becomes impossible for anyone to take it away because it's simply in me.

Knowing your weakness: One of the strategies that will help you have perfect inner peace is to discover your weaknesses, work on improving them, and become a better person. The reason why many people are easily defeated is because they allow people to easily spot their weaknesses. When people know your weakness, they tend to capitalize on that, and they easily use it against you. The victim doesn't often realize it, but that wouldn't stop him from asking himself the question, why is this person doing this to me?

In fact, they often ask such questions, and this tends to disturb their inner peace in the long run. So, the best thing to do in such circumstances is to start working on your weakness. You can only do this when you know or spot your weakness. Having a weakness will always lead to an inner peace imbalance because when you give out peace to others, you will be expecting peace in return. You may not get it if people tend to use your weakness against you or pay you back with a bad attitude simply because they know you are weak. For instance, I have a friend who is very humble and has a gentle-like manner. Each time there is a fight, he tries to settle it. People who know him very well know he is a peace-loving person. But he has some young men who often like to bully him. They know he is a peaceful and gentle person, but they can't help bullying him because they already know that he won't fight back.

The lesson here is that you don't necessarily have to settle every dispute by actions; there are better ways you can pass a message across without having to participate in actions. Words can speak louder than actions sometimes. The Buddhist mindfulness can be accomplished with words to express issues, and mere words, if properly applied, can win the heart. Yes, I know that actions can speak louder than words, and that ideology is action-based. But words can be so powerful that they can bring tears to the eyes of many people, while mere actions can bring tears to the eyes of one person. This can be achieved through Buddhism. Once you are able to influence people with abilities such as these, you can change everything around you.

Happiness: Being happy gives you inner peace, so whatever comes your way, whether it is good or bad, always learn to be happy. If you have a problem that seems to defy every solution, this can cause an imbalance in your inner peace. This is because you will always be thinking about the problems, and your mind will not be at rest. It creates an imbalance in your innermost being. It's okay, everyone has problems, and if that problem is not solved in the present, it will be solved later. Don't let problems bother you. Instead, let your peace of mind take control of the situation. From the beginning of the world, there have always been problems. We came into this world to meet problems; there are so many problems. If we let problems stop us from being humans or concentrate all our efforts thinking about the problems of the world, we would never get anywhere in life. Therefore, leave the problem or find a solution to it. There is no problem without a solution. When there is no solution, the problems can be kept where they are until you find a solution for them.

Therefore, problems shouldn't steal away your happiness. You did not create the problem. And even if you did, you can always find a solution. But if you can't, let it be, especially if it doesn't affect you directly.

Rest of Mind: If you really want inner peace, always make efforts to have rest of mind, let your mind be at rest. Let your mind be at rest with everyone around you; your neighbors, family members, colleagues at work, friends at school, course mates, people in your political circle, and those in the same or different religion with you. Why give yourself so much pain and trouble with a restless mind? If you have issues or misunderstandings with anyone, settle it. You can always make peace by discussing issues with someone you have a misunderstanding with. You have to allow your mind to be at rest with everyone. That is how to maintain inner peace. You have to be peaceful with yourself and the people around you. So always try to allow your mind to be at rest and don't have any grudges against anyone.

Smile: "Smile" is one of the simplest five-letter words yet so powerful. A smile can change a lot of things about you. No matter the circumstances you find yourself, smile. "Smile" is the most powerful five-letter word that exists. Why? Because when you smile positively, nobody actually knows what you are going through. A smile radiates friendship, it attracts people to you. A person who was keeping words to himself can easily open up to you simply because of the smile on your face. The truth is; a smile always creates something in your spirit that enables you to see through things that others wouldn't see. You need to understand that a simple smile can turn things around for good. For instance, a certain man was embarking on a journey. He had prepared so well; he arranged his luggage, locked his door, and went off to the road. Then something happened, but he wasn't aware. He lost his keys as he was travelling. He checked his pockets when he got to a point, and he wasn't happy that he couldn't find his keys after searching everywhere.

He was so sad; he started tracing his steps and searching through the path he had traveled. He came across a man who was also traveling along the same path with his dog. The dog had discovered a bunch of keys and ran to it and started barking. The owner came close to the dog, picked up the keys, and placed them in his pocket. A little while later, he continued his journey, and he met the owner of the keys on the road. The man and his dog greeted the man, but he was so sad that he didn't reply since he was looking for his keys. However, the dog kept barking at him. The owner of the dog asked after they had passed each other a few steps, "Are you looking for something?" He replied, "I just lost my keys." While the dog was still barking, the man brought out the keys and handed them over to him, and then he smiled.

The lesson you should learn here is, no matter the circumstances, you should always smile. If not for the dog, the man wouldn't have found his keys. Secondly, he refused to answer a greeting, which would have saved him the stress of having to go miles still searching for his keys. At the point of greeting, the problem of the missing keys would have been solved. Always learn to smile. Smiling will bring solutions to problems. You will not get solutions to problems when you are sad or confused; the solution can only come when you are smiling. Most people find it difficult to smile; I wish they could understand that there are so many benefits of smiling. A smile is so powerful that it transcends the ordinary state of life.

It's a natural phenomenon that creates the balance in inner peace when you go through some difficulty, yet you remain stable and unaffected by what you are going through. A smile is the key to a greater inner peace, more than you can ever imagine. Although the problem may be there, you don't have to make the problem your priority. Make smiling your priority and relegate the problem to the background where it should be. Of course, among your list of activities for the day or week, let problems which you cannot solve, they are placed apart from your priorities. This is because problems can sometimes hold you back from making progress. So if problems are stopping you from making progress, keep them away from your daily activities. I am sure you will find a solution to them somehow.

Stop worrying: A lot of people worry about things that happen in their lives, especially if the going is not good. They tend to be sad, and they worry about the things that bother them. Let me tell you something, the moment you begin to worry about the disturbing issues in your life, that is when you begin to develop health issues. When you worry too much about certain matters in your life, you begin to develop depression. It gradually sets in because your mood is changing, and it starts to influence the inner peace that you have. Then you get agitated or anticipate and see things in a different way. When you worry, it affects the mind; remember a mind is a powerful tool that helps your development. Your mind will not function well because you worry too much.

Worrying affects the mind; take, for example, a man who is driving a car, but is worried about his responsibilities. He has to pay school fees; his rent has expired; he doesn't have the money to take care of his family, and so on. Of course, these are issues that are of great concern. They are pressing needs that need to be addressed, but do you have to worry about them all the time? No! The man doesn't have to worry about those problems; all he needs to do is seek solutions to those problems.

There are different ways to take care of your worries. The best way is to prioritize the issues that need to be taken care of in order of their importance. Which one is more important and needs immediate attention? That's how it ought to be done, taking the issues one by one. If your rent is what you need to pay first, find a solution to that first. If it is the children's school fees that need to be taken care of, handle it first before any other problem. That's how to make things work. If you consider these points, you will begin to develop a balanced inner peace. This is because you will have nothing to worry about when you are able to take every issue one after the other. If you cannot find the solution to a problem, then why do you have to worry about such a problem? If worrying doesn't solve it, then why worry?

Good Health: You need to develop a way of staying healthy with regular checks. Health is wealth; the number one thing that is key to a successful innermost peace is to have good and sound health. Don't mistake always having good food to eat to mean having good health. No! To be healthy doesn't necessarily mean you should have money to buy any type of food you want. Staying healthy means you eat the right food and also give yourself mental and spiritual food, not just physical food. Make yourself physically fit so that you will be able to concentrate on the practice of self-development and advancement. Buddhist student needs to stay healthy. All your physical components need to be working well so that you are able to study, live in the system, and maximize the benefits. Your inner peace is important if you have to create the balance you need to stay healthy. If you are sick, you will not be able to practice some abstinence rules or obligations. When you need to remain focused and concentrate for hours, removing yourself from the physical world and off to the advanced innermost self-world where you will see beyond the ordinary self, you must stay healthy. Not being healthy may affect your progress, and this will never bring great inner peace.

Anger Management

Anger is a strong annoyance that generates from the inside of a person. Sometimes anger can become a problem, and this often leads to so many setbacks in a person's life. To manage and overcome your anger, you need to learn from the system of the Buddhist who is capable of controlling his anger through a well laid down procedure. Anger is simply unhealthy, especially in the home, among people, at school, a working environment, in the market, in politics, and in any human interaction. Anger is a very bad attribute that can lead to destruction and disharmony. Lots of people in the world today are unable to control their anger, and this has led to many downfalls for them.

I understand that people have different temperaments; your ability to control your anger may be different from the ability of another person. However, anger can be managed if you follow the right steps to guide you to change from being an overly angry person to a whole new person with a reduced temperament. Anger causes bad health for an individual who is always angry. Getting rid of anger may be very difficult, but in most people, it never goes away. They are so used to getting angry at the slightest provocation. Time is needed for some people with anger issues to get healing. For some people, getting angry is not a problem. They hardly get angry, but when they do, it can be dangerous because they will release all the anger in them since they are not used to releasing it immediately. This often leads to transferred aggression, which makes people wonder if this person has been pretending all along. So now the question is, how can you manage your anger? I'm sure you are interested in the Buddhist way of handling anger.

Shift Your Mind towards Something Else: Anger often comes when you get offended by somebody. The person has offended you and perhaps is too arrogant to apologize to you. This might piss you off, and you feel it's not right; not everybody can take an insult and swallow it. But you can get over anger by just shifting your attention towards something else. Taking your mind off the offense that someone committed against you and directing your mind towards something else is one of the major keys to becoming successful in managing your anger. However, this is based on offenses committed against you by another person. On the other hand, if you have an inner problem of anger, there are other ways you can achieve successful anger management.

Showing Love: One of the most potent ways of managing your anger is to show love irrespective of the fact that you have been hurt by somebody. Love cures and heals anger in a way that you may not understand. When you constantly show love to people, you are able to show a better understanding that you have a mature mind. Even if you are young, you can be a better person when you show love in situations that bring about anger. If you are a loving person and are able to show love to every person that comes your way, irrespective of race, color, or gender, you will be better able to manage your anger. This is because anger comes from the heart, and if you have a loving heart, mind, soul, and body, you will show less anger towards people.

Tolerance: A lot of people find it difficult to tolerate other people, especially when it comes to behaviors that are unethical to society's standards. They tend to hate such people and are unable to stand their presence. No matter what people do to you, you need to learn how to tolerate them. The Buddhist student learns this and gains understanding and knowledge on how to deal with people with different characteristics or behavioral dispositions. "To tolerate" means that you are able to accept people the way they are irrespective of their social class. Do not attempt to segregate or make people believe that they are worthless even when they know they have fallen short of normally acceptable standards. If you meet a poor person, always try to understand that the person is poor and needs help. People are poor not because of their own fault, but perhaps they have not gotten the right opportunity to flourish. You can become a leading light and show them the path to success. This can only be achieved if you show tolerance towards them.

Withdrawal Method: The withdrawal method is based on the fact that when you are annoyed by any individual, all you do is walk away. This has been found over the years to be very effective in anger management processes. The Buddhist student understands that there are a lot of benefits when he decides to withdraw himself from the trouble zone, especially when there is a heated argument. You decide to withdraw yourself from that scenario, not because you are a coward or you cannot fight back, but because you want to maintain peace within yourself and with others. And because you don't want anything that will get you angry, you just decide to walk away from the trouble. This is one of the most effective ways of managing your anger. If you can do this often, as many times as possible, you will be able to get over your frequent state of being angry.

Self-Control: Self-control is very useful when you are annoyed. It is the ability to control yourself when you get angry or when someone annoys you. Not many people in the world have self-control. One of the pillars of the Buddhist student to be successful is to have self-control. No matter what the situation is, if it makes you flare up, you can control it by simply refusing to get moved into arguments or fights. Self-control in any situation is very important because, in most cases, it is during anger situations that vital information is released. If you get angry, you won't be able to get it. Self-control enables you to read the mind of your opponent or antagonist. Whatever he says to you, you remain silent, and you'll be able to digest and read his mind through the words that come out from his mouth. The Buddhist understands the teaching concerning anger management and self-control because he remotely absents his human nature from the presence of the chaotic situation. Anger assumes a chaotic position because it starts from an individual's inside to his outside. A Buddhist student is always well aware of this and works towards self-control, which is the hallmark of Buddhist practice. Hardly does a Buddhist react immediately to an angry situation. There is a lot to learn from being still and maintaining self-control during such a situation. As a Buddhist student, this is the point of call where you will need self-control.

Our daily lifestyle in modern society enables us to interact with people. You will need to understand the true meaning of self-control in most situations because as long as you interact with people, the chances that you will get into conflict are high. You need to develop the characteristics to really maintain self-control because it will always be necessary.

Don't Let Fear Control Your Life

Fear is when an individual is afraid of something. That thing can be connected or may not be connected to an individual. That is why there is the fear of the unknown and the fear of whatever is bothering you. Some philosophers have defined "FEAR" as "false evidence appearing real." This is true because what you conceive in your mind is often what you get. If you are afraid of something, that thing will eventually consume you and defeat you. When you are living in fear, it means you have allowed it to control your life. This is not healthy for your senses, mind, soul, as well as your physical and spiritual development. The Buddhist practice is far ahead in defeating fear because Buddhists are not controlled by it. The mind is capable of many things, depending on what it is fed with. When you permit fear to control your life, you have fallen already because fear comes before a downfall. Many people in the world today actually live in fear of what is going to happen to them in the next minute or later in the future.

There are various reasons people live in fear. For instance, if there is no job for a person, he may become afraid of financial security. Where will he get money to buy the necessities of life, and how will he survive? How will he get money to take care of his family? As long as he doesn't have a job, a business to make money, a source of income or livelihood, the fear of financial security will always be an issue. Until he gets a job, that fear will never leave him.

Another instance; the doctors say you have a problem with your liver or kidney, and you may die at any moment. You end up living in fear of death; that is exactly what is happening to some people in the world today. We have seen people, especially rich people, build fences around their homes and houses, and the fences are sometimes even taller than prison yard fences. They are so afraid; they think someone is after them or is coming to hurt them.

This is the fear of the unknown, but if you are living a good life and are not against anyone, you will live peacefully with everyone around you. Why should you be afraid of something happening to you? There is no need to fear. It often leads to unnecessary panic because your mind will be made up of fear. Any alarm, even when it is false, makes you afraid. This shouldn't be your mindset; don't be fearful about whatever you are doing. Fear has never helped anybody and will not help you either. Somehow, fear has a way of connecting with the nature of a man. When a man lives his life in fear, he becomes timid, in every (circumstance) he becomes afraid of what faces him. Don't let fear control your life, and for you to overcome fear, you need the following attributes:

Courage: You need courage whenever you are faced with difficulty in life. Being courageous enough to face difficult situations and overcome them is very important as you live your life daily. Courage is the ability to face whatever situation or circumstances that come your way without fear. The Buddhist is always courageous to overcome that which threatens his mind. Self-encouragement can be attained by lots of Buddhist practice. The inspiration of the Buddhist religion is essential to the Buddhist because he is able to draw comfort, energy, and courage from the innermost gifts that he has. Courage is also essential in facing difficult moments, and you can only be able to achieve it when you are well-prepared through Buddhist religious practices. The higher level of spirituality and tradition goes a long way to help in the mental development of a timid person if he is fearful, making him leave the fearful life behind him.

The motivation of the mind: One thing that is very effective in changing a fearful life is motivation. When you are motivated, you can defeat your fear. What is required is the "Yes, I can" attitude. Always see yourself as capable of defeating any difficult situation. Anything that comes your way can always be defeated, it is your choice. The Buddhist is always motivated and will make no excuses when it comes to instances of being fearful. The more the challenges come, the more the Buddhist with his understanding will be motivated to face such challenges or difficulty. You can only draw motivation from your inner self if your mind is prepared. But if your mind is not prepared, you will always get negative responses even if you try. Fortunately, the Buddhist practice will help you out in any type of situation. Motivation to defeat fear may not come from the outside, it has to come from within yourself. It may be difficult to achieve it if you have been used to living a fearful life. Hence, you must admit that you need help which can be availed to you through the Buddhist practice. When you get hold of it and practice it successfully, you will overcome your fear. Fear may come from your work, school, or your environment. You may get threats often from people who don't like you, and the external factor, fear, is giving you problems when it comes from the outside. But when fear comes from the inside, it will give you self-defeat. It's better not to allow yourself to be defeated, you are a champion, and that is the kind of mindset that you should always carry.

Fear controls your life like a human will control a robot. You are not a robot, you were created by a higher source of spirituality, and you are a gift to the world. No psychological stance, set of beliefs, or mindset level that fear holds against you can defeat you. That shouldn't be. Another thing that is responsible for fear ruling your life that you should be aware of or get rid of is the "inferiority complex." People have certain levels of inferiority complex, which is based on the belief that they are not better than the other person. It may be because of your skin color, your mindset, or you think others are better than you in certain circumstances of life. Then you begin to fathom some kind of fantasy around their greatness. You see yourself as someone less worthy than they are, but this is a false belief system that you should not be harboring at all. The first thing that you should always have at the back of your mind is that nobody is greater than you. We are all equal but may have different gifts.

To avoid living in fear of being inferior to others, you need to develop what is referred to as "self-identification of a gift." This system of thinking and self-discovery enables you to discover your own special gift and talent and develop it for better improvement of your personality. Nobody can stop you from becoming what you want to become, and that is why your destiny is tied to something that is worth your life. Your life is special, which is why you live among men. The moment you start thinking towards this direction, the better a person you become. Although we are created with different gifts and talents, we can always identify the gifts and talents that we have. This can be achieved by the practice of self-reflection and re-examination, through the Buddhist spirituality and system of religion.

Over 400 million people who practice Buddhism have discovered how useful it is to defeat fear. This is because of the indebtedness of the level of spirituality, which has led to the discovery of self and instant change in the level of mindfulness. In turn, this has led to great transformation among individuals who practice Buddhism. The knowledge and wisdom gained through the practice have made lots of people benefit from the processes of Buddhism.

In this modern society, you definitely need the spiritual tradition of the Buddhist, which tremendously enhances the state of mind of an individual. The moment has come for you to work on your fears. Through the Buddhist religious practice and spirituality, you will overcome your greatest fears and no longer allow fear to control your life anymore.

How to Overcome Serious Hardship & Adversity

Hardship is when a person is going through some difficult and trying moments in life. There are basically three different faces of hardship. Hardship can come; naturally, it can be self-inflicted, or it can be caused by a third party.

People all over the world go through some levels of hardship, which can come in many ways. It usually falls within the three categories aforementioned. Some people tend to give up whenever they face hardship. They find it difficult to deal with life, are usually upset and give up whenever they can no longer bear the hardship. We have people who are capable of enduring hardship for a longer period of time until they finally overcome it. While we also have people who endure hardship and die in that hardship, which may not necessarily be what they wish for themselves but because they have no way out, it leaves them helpless.

Naturally, a person can have difficulty in life as a result of the circumstances of his birth. A person may be born blind, so the hardship that such a person will be facing is the ability to see. Another example is if a person is born with a deformity, he may be unable to walk for the rest of his life. There are so many instances. Serious hardship can come from these circumstances of birth, which usually leave many in a difficult situation in trying to get the best out of life. Yet, we have seen some people with deformity who have decided to claim that there is "ability in disability" and are able to turn their disability into ability with great achievements recorded in the history of the world. You can also have serious hardship getting pregnant as a married woman. Your husband or many people around you will think you are barren. Some may become abusive that you cannot get pregnant, but this is absolutely not true. The fact that they said so doesn't mean you cannot overcome such difficulty.

You may have started a business, and you feel your business is not doing well. After investing so much into it, your business is still not doing as well as you wanted it to. You run into debts, you can't meet the demands of your clients and customers, and you become very sad about the way things are playing out. Your business is not making profit, instead, you are operating at a loss. This is a very serious hardship because you need to pay staff salaries but you are owing them. So in the face of these kinds of hardship, how do you manage to overcome them? Perhaps you are a student, you want to go to school and get an education, but your parents cannot afford a higher education for you. You wanted to become an engineer but you are unable to achieve your dreams. What's going to be your next action? Will you just allow the difficulty to swallow you up, or start something, or figure a way out of the situation? When you learn and practice Buddhism, it will direct you on the path of success, the path of taking you out of problems. Solutions are developed through the inner virtue that radiates from the inside, empowering you to get one step ahead of advancement against anything that will pose hardship in your life.

Adversity is a misfortune that usually brings hardship to people. Misfortune can be a disease. When you are infected with a disease that seems to defy all forms of curative measures taken against it by a doctor or health practitioner, you begin to lose hope. That is a misfortune. You may be involved in an accident and feel very bad about it because you sustained grievous injuries. This is another way in which you can begin to suffer hardship. You can be bedridden in the hospital for months, medical bills keep piling up, and you are unable to pay. This is another thing that brings hardship.

You got out of the university after your years of study, but have been unable to secure a job. You feel life is treating you badly, and you feel like giving up. Your parents want you to get a job and move on with life or even take care of your immediate siblings. You feel like a failure because you don't have money. Now, you need to consider the fact that hardship is there which cannot be ignored. It is real, yet you can actually turn your hardship or adversity into success. This is the only way you are going to get over it.

Identify the Causes of Hardship and Adversity: It is very important to learn and detect the causes of adversity or hardship. The first thing that is necessary for you to get over hardship is to identify the source or causes of it. This is so important because it is based on practical identification of the root causes of hardship. The process can vary from one type of situation to another. What is obtainable in the urban area may be different from what you would get in a rural area. The hardship that has to do with traveling through a long-distance where you don't have a vehicle, for instance, is easily identifiable. This is because you don't have a vehicle and you need to travel a long distance. You know there is a hardship or difficult situation that limits your movement. Hence you identified the hardship. What you can do is figure out how to get a vehicle to take you through the journey.

Look for a Solution: When you have hardship in your life, it usually tends to make you look for a solution or a way out. Allowing hardship to persist will only make you tired. Many people in the world today are tired already because they are unable to get solutions to their hardship or adversity. The first thing you should do in the face of adversity or serious hardship is to look for lasting solutions to the hardship that you are facing. Solutions can start from within you, following the Buddhist system of practice. Every solution to a problem can start from the inner self. When you provide solutions for the inner self, you will get the needed or right solution to the hardship that you are facing. This is because the conviction you have that you can provide the solution to the hardship can lead you to get the solution from the outside. That is if you are able to get the necessary solution from the inside.

Solutions to hardship vary from one individual to another, and using the Buddhist practice on self-spirituality takes you away from it. Like, the pioneers of Buddhist practice usually leave a troubled zone to a safe and quiet atmosphere where they can concentrate on the development of solutions to their hardship or what they were facing. This usually leads them to an advanced realm of knowledge and understanding of how the solution to problems can be attained. And this is through a higher level of spirituality based on a practiced tradition that has proven to bring success.

Taking control and being in control of the situation is always worth it because it means that you are in charge. Not allowing the adversity to dictate the life that you live or dictate what will happen to you next is like fighting a battle. You resist the hardship from affecting you. Sometimes the hardship may take a toll on you, but you are resolute in making sure that you are going to win the battle. This is a form of self-thought. It goes into your subconscious mind through fighting what you are going through, and definitely, when you adopt the Buddhist system of consciousness and inner discipline, you will always conquer.

Resilience: Being resilient in times of hardship is something that you can actually start practicing and achieve. To be resilient means that you refuse to allow your hardship to put you down. You develop a stubborn spirit. Even if the hardship knocks you down several, you keep getting back up.

To be resilient can be seen in a scenario where a very big dog living in a rich man's house is guarding the house. It has rich food, the big dog is well taken care of, but there was this smaller dog who usually comes around from the street. The smaller dog lived in a very small house, and it desired the food and the kind of house the big dog was staying in. Every day, the smaller dog will come to the big dog's compound, and the big dog will try to scare it away. It always involves a fight, and the smaller dog, after being defeated, will just walk away but still return the next day for a fight. It kept on doing this daily until the bigger dog got tired and left the house for the smaller dog.

So you see, when you are resilient, just like the smaller dog, there will always be a final solution. And often, the result will be positive because you kept on working on how to get rid of the hardship. This same thing is what happens in real life. Those who are resilient in the face of hardship always come out victorious.

Persistence: Persistence is when you keep doing things positively that you know or learned will get rid of the hardship. If you want to bring down a tree with an ax, and if it's going to take you 8 hours, it means you have to use 4 hours to sharpen your ax. This means you have to prepare and carry on the course by being persistent. You have to spend and maximize the 8 hours to chop down the tree. But before that can happen, you have to do the necessary things, being persistent is one of them.

Consistent: You have to be consistent when you are trying to solve adversity. Putting an end to particular adversity that is inflicting pain on you means you have to be consistent. The Buddhist system of religion teaches about consistency, especially in its way of life. The Buddhist never changes or compromises his position to lower the standard of his ancient tradition and religion. This is why you need to understand what it means to be consistent. Being consistent in the face of hardship will prove how strong you are both mentally, physically, spiritually, and mindfully.

If you looked around you today in the world, there are people who are not consistent. We have people who are jacks of all trade, but in actual fact, they are masters of none. That's why you may see people in one particular profession, and they seem not to like what they are doing and deviate to another profession. I've seen football stars who, after playing football, got interested in some other sport like basketball or racing, and sometimes we ask, do they really know what they are doing? To be consistent means you are doing things constantly within the same profession, and you attain a level of excellence because you understand and have gathered experience in that profession. The time comes for the experience to pay off and not dabbling into a new profession by starting all over again.

If you are in MMA sports, for instance, and you are doing excellently well without being defeated, why not spend your entire career there and retire? Why divert to boxing where you don't have the experience or longevity in the sport? You will only end up losing at the end of the day, and that is not a wise decision. If you are good at mathematics, you can develop very well in that area. Why abandon it for another thing which is totally different from the calculation? A Buddhist has a high level of concentration and is always consistent with whatever he is doing. That is why Buddhists are known for being unchanged in their performance from time immemorial. Consistency will make you defeat your adversity period.

Turn Your Hardship into Success: The problem with most people is their inability to transform or convert their adversity into success. When you know you have something that is making you not to move on with your life, and it becomes disturbing, you know you have to do something about it to get out of the situation. All you need to do is turn the hardship into success. I will tell you a story about a young boy who was in school; he came from a poor family, and he was a very skinny boy. When he went to school, there was another boy who was bigger, but just a little taller than the skinny boy. The big boy noticed how skinny the other boy was and always bullied him because he knew he could beat him up. Whenever the skinny boy gets something to eat, the big boy comes around and takes it away from him, and says, "It's mine now, so what are you going to do?" The skinny boy just cries and leaves; he couldn't fight. One day he was passing through a boxing club, and he saw some young lads going in. He walked into the boxing club, and an elderly man who was a veteran and boxing coach noticed him. He was wondering what could have brought the boy into the boxing club. He observed the little skinny boy walk to the gym and sit down, watching other boys in training.

He was sad, but, the elderly man noticed that the skinny boy was staring at how the boys were boxing. When they had left, the skinny boy went and stood close to the punching bag and threw a punch, but the resulting effect made him fall on the floor. And he felt he was never going to learn how to fight. But the elderly man went to him and stretched out his hand. The boy grabbed it, and he pulled him up, then the elderly man said to him, "I think you are going to be a great boxer one day, come on."

The elderly man gave the skinny boy a card and an appointment for free classes. To cut the story short, the skinny boy went on to become a world champion after ten years of graduating from school. He had lost contact with the big boy until one day after his boxing match, which he had won, he was heading back home, and someone stopped him and asked for a favor. Behold, it was the big boy who used to bully the skinnier boy, who is now a world boxing champion. The big boy was asking for money, he had no job after school, and he went into the streets. He didn't recognize the skinny boy anymore. But the skinny boy recognized him, called out his name, and reminded him of how he used to bully him back then in school. So the big boy who had lost his frame was ashamed and knelt down begging. He was thinking the skinny boy would beat him up because he was now a professional boxer and of course the big boy couldn't fight with him. The skinny boy told him to get up, that he wasn't going to hurt him. But he said something which was striking. The skinny boy said, "Thank you for showing me my path to life. Because you bullied me back in school, I began to learn how to fight, and it's because of you I am a world champion now."

This is exactly what should happen to you when you are faced with hardship and adversity. All you need to do is figure out a way of changing your circumstances and making it work for you. Many people find themselves in similar situations; the problem is they don't make the right move in the right direction to solve their problems or adversity.

Turning your obstacles to stepping stones: The Buddhist approach to adversity is simply the fact that if you follow the teachings and apply it in your daily life, you will be able to change your circumstances, especially when you face hardship. Converting your serious hardships into success is what you will do to achieve success as a Buddhist. Because it is based on ancient teachings that have worked for those who practice it, when you feel overwhelmed by your hardships, see it as something that is going to make you greater in the future. You can actually become stronger by the challenges that your hardship present to you because they will push you to become successful. Without hardship, lots of people out there will not be successful or become stronger. But because they have been made to pass through hardship, they learn through the experience. Hardship presents to us a way of learning new things in the face of difficulty. Behind every cloud, there is always a silver lining, and when you believe this adage, you will understand that your suffering or hardship will only propel you to success.

Best Strategies To Healing Yourself

The best strategies to healing yourself is very wide teaching that is basically based on personal experience and relationships with other people. So many people in the world are affected by the activities of other people. There is sadness, unhappiness, greed, pain, jealousy, conflicts, disagreements, unforgiveness, scheming, plotting others' downfall, etc. The list is endless, as many people are not satisfied with what they are getting out of life. There are lots of people suffering around the world. The process of healing the world has been discussed in the last two decades by a notable musician who sang about healing the world. But how can we heal the world when people don't have peace, and every man has not gotten the right enlightenment? Healing the world begins with an individual. It spreads, and until we all begin to develop the mindfulness of healing each other and actually implementing it, the world will still remain the same.

The process of healing has been developed over the years; there are various instances where people need healing. Basically, the question is, who needs healing? What readily comes to mind if you are going to answer such a question is the thought of a person who is sick. But the truth of the matter is that everybody needs healing; the earth needs healing, anything that has life needs healing, and that is the bitter truth. When we talk about healing, it is all-encompassing; therefore, I will take you through the various aspects of healing.

Healing the Earth: Following the teaching about what you sow is what you reap; for instance, if you cultivate land and go planting crops during the planting season, during the harvest you will reap the harvest of what you cultivated. If you plant yams, you will reap yams; if you plant potatoes, you will reap potatoes. You cannot plant maize and harvest rice, it's not possible. What am I trying to say here? The interpretation here is that what you feed your mind is what you will get, and this is exactly why people who take drugs will have the side effects of such drugs. Taking hard drugs will lead to drug abuse, and drinking alcohol frequently will make you form the habit. This can equally lead to alcoholism problems and other problems associated with depression. Now that we have established the fact that there are things we do to ourselves that cause us illness let's go further into other instances where we need healing.

Human illnesses: If an individual is sick, definitely such an individual needs healing because an illness is also a way of suffering. Not only will you not be feeling fine, but you can be bedridden in the hospital as a result of suffering. So, a person who is sick needs healing, and to get the person healed completely, he needs to undergo some therapy or treatment. This may lead to the prescription of medication to aid the recovery of such an individual. In the same way, we all need to get healing through a process. Therefore, to get healing, you will need to submit yourself and allow treatment to take place so you can get the healing that will restore you to good health. The healing process starts with a physician who is well skilled and trained in administering healing on a sick person. The doctor or physician carries out medical examination on such an individual and prescribes the medicine or starts the healing process. This is how the healing process for a sick person is achieved.

In the same way, we need healing in our lives. Every daily activity that we partake in or carry out affects us. But there are other aspects of healing that are meant to give us spiritual cleansing and transformation both mentally, physically, and mindfully. Before we can understand or become open to the process, we must stick to these tenets for the total healing to take place in us, and they are:

Forgive and forget: Forgiveness is the ability to forgive people when they offend you. No matter the number of times a person offends you, you must learn how to forgive such people. It is in forgiving that we can let go of the pain and grudge, and then we will find happiness. We cannot be happy when we have people in mind, people who have hurt us. They may know, or they may not even know, so it bears no pain in them.

They may be unaware that they have hurt us either with their words or actions or omissions. Yet, we feel angry about it, even when they are not aware of the offense they committed against us, so who is in pain? It's you, of course! Because you carry the offense in your mind and you have not learned to let go, you feel pain each time you see the person that offended you. You are not at peace with yourself. You have to forgive that person and forget about the pain he caused you.

Embrace Dialogue: Human interactions are not void of conflicts and misunderstanding. As long as we are living in the world, we will always have situations and circumstances when we will have a disagreement. The best thing to do in such circumstances is to try to have a conversation with the person who offended you. Have a heart-to-heart discussion, talk to the person about what he has done, and see if he is aware or not. Because sometimes, people who offend us may not be aware that they did. Secondly, whether the person apologizes or not, you can end the problem with dialogue and don't allow it to linger. There is no issue that cannot be discussed and resolved, so always make efforts to be the one ready and open to dialogue. This way, you will not allow the problem to spread further and go beyond the resolution. You will be satisfied that you brought the topic up and that the issue has been resolved. This way, it is a healing for both parties.

Show Compassion: Be a compassionate human being. When you are filled with compassion, you will always be noticed. And you can be referred to as a true peaceful human being who has a human face even in the face of difficulty. There are those who need people to reach out to them, but they are not getting people to show compassion to them. Living a life of compassion in itself is a healing that is beyond compare because you are touching lives, and you have the tendency to be a compassionate human being who cares about the suffering of other people.

Show Kindness: Kindness is something that attracts blessings. If you are kind to people, you will, in the end, get help from an unknown source. It happens because you started deeds that draw and attract nature. When you bless people, the universe will connive and bless you too; it is the law of attraction. Kindness will always attract wonderful things to your life. The more you show kindness, the greater the tendency that you become happy with yourself. This is also a form of healing for your mind.

Detaching yourself from Materialism: Materialism is overtly showing love for modern things of the world.

Perhaps you are so attached to living in a mansion; you want to drive the latest cars, you love flashy cars, you want to travel around the world, you want to play for the best clubs, and there are so many desires. Of course, these are wonderful things in life, and it is great to have them, they give us great comfort. But what if you don't have the money to buy them? What if your income is too low to afford a mansion or a flashy car? The chances that you will not be happy are high in such circumstances. This may bring great discomfort, making you feel bad about it, and in this case, you need healing.

You need to understand that sometimes life is not a bed of roses. We are born, and we all have a destiny. Understand that there is suffering in life; there are ends and a path to the end of suffering. If we attach ourselves to these material things, they will give us a bad feeling if we do not have them, which may even affect our health. That's an unhealthy lifestyle; you need to learn how to detach yourself from all things that are capable of taking away your happiness or making you sad if you don't have them. When you start thinking in that direction, you will receive healing.

Love Yourself: We have people in the world who find it difficult to love themselves. But before you can get healing, you need to start by loving yourself. A lack of self-love is unhealthy and will definitely make you unhappy. The best way to start loving yourself is to make efforts to admit that you have weaknesses, and these weaknesses can be corrected. Don't see others as better human beings than you are. Everyone is unique according to their capabilities and gifts. The fact is that all human beings have the same fate i.e., aging, illness, and death. Not seeing yourself as lesser of a human being than any other person will make you free from what can affect your mind when you are tempted to compare yourself with others.

Don't compare yourself with any other person: living a normal life is not competing with people, but being yourself. Don't live your life trying to compete with others. True happiness and healing are not achieved when you are competing with other people. Rather, when you live peacefully without involving yourself in any form of competition, this will enable you to get real healing. There are times when there is competition staring you in the face. This happens if we engage in some form of discipline. For instance, if you are a sportsperson, or you are given targets by your employer, or you have contemporaries in the same business. Or when there is a position that opens in the company, you want to apply for such position or post, and you have other candidates who are fighting to get such positions too; these are situations where you will be faced with competition. For the last one, you don't need to get involved in competition with anyone who is trying to outsmart you in getting into positions. Avoid occasions where you will have to compete with others to get something. This is a form of attachment that will always affect your happiness. When you have situations where you are not happy, you gradually get sick, and then you will need healing to get out of that situation.

Contentment: Be content with what you have. When what you have is not much, and others have more than you, there is the temptation to desire what other people have in terms of possession and wealth. Don't always try to have what others have. With that kind of mindset, you will have problems with your mental disposition, and if you can't get what they have, you begin to fall sick both physically, mentally, and emotionally. This will cause a negative impact on your health and your mind, which may make you jealously sick. When you are in such a situation, you really need help and healing. Avoid being so interested in possessing what others have that you don't. Be satisfied with what you have at the moment, work towards a better future, and you will surely get it. Always remember that there is a time for everything.

Your time will come when you will be able to get those things that you really need.

Devote time for quiet Moments: Healing begins with an individual's effort to get well. Healing is not all about outward signs of assistance that can be gotten from a physician; it also has to do with something from the inside of an individual. Many people have ill-health not because they have not eaten well, but because they have never once in many years sat down to reflect on the life that they are living. Sometimes you need to go out to an environment where you can be alone and meditate on the things happening around you. And sometimes you need to take your mind off things that are giving you so much trouble. Develop a positive mindset, a mind free of troubles, and worries of this world. You need a quiet moment to yourself, a time you can be alone and reflect on the past, present, and future. This is a great path to a healing process that comes from the inside.

Change your circle of friends: Show me your friends, and I will tell you who you are; this saying is what has long been known to reveal the kind of person an individual is through the types of friends he or she is keeping. Now what this implies is that sometimes in our lives, the kinds of friends we keep may not be true friends but "fair-weather friends." They are with you because of what they are gaining from you. Maybe they are benefiting from what you have. You may have money to spend on your friends, so partying and enjoying the comfort of your house and presence is what they are after. Once you have a problem, they will simply disappear. And you will begin to wonder if you really had them as friends, or they were just interested in what they were gaining from you. You will be surprised to find that you don't have any friends. This can make you feel bad, and when you remember them, you tend to feel angry. The best advice is for you to change your circle of friends. And when you start gaining friends that are responsible and true, you will feel much better. When you have friends who are like-minded, friends who share your dream, and your kind of mindset, you will feel better having them around you. Rather than friends who are just interested in what they can gain from you and not how they can help you achieve your dreams.

Be in a Healthy Relationship: If you want to experience healing, be in a healthy and good relationship with a person whose qualities you are very familiar with. Not everybody can be your perfect match, but you can get someone who is the perfect match for you. All you need to do is study and take your time to find that person. Many people get into relationships that they end up regretting, and this usually causes an emotional breakdown. When the relationship is broken, they find it difficult to move on. For some people, it may be easy, but for some other individuals, it may take time, while some never forget the person who broke their heart, and that is a fact. It is hard to forget the first person, friend, or partner who broke your heart when you were in a relationship with him or her. So this makes us think a lot, and it always comes with many regrets. We begin to think, "How I wish the relationship did not end," "How I wish I could turn back the hands of the clock," and so on. We have people who find it very difficult to recover from the various bad relationships they had, and this has also led to psychological trauma. It's sad to see people suffer from such conditions. The real deal is this; when this happens to you, yes you may be heartbroken, yes I understand that you have been hurt, but it's okay, life goes on. You are worth more than a broken heart, and you should move on with your life. The future is always bigger and greater than what happened in the past because what awaits you is bigger than what happened to you in the past.

Have you ever thought of why life has been developing and improving ever since human beings came into existence? Have you? Definitely, it's a known fact that, at a point in time, there were no airplanes to fly from one continent to the other in just a few hours. There were no ships to move cargoes or goods from one country or seashore to another, and there were no billionaires. But what do we have today? We have the sophistication, high mental development, higher technological advancement, and the best facilities that support human lives. The information age is awesome, to be able to communicate with a person from one continent to another. This is why we believe that the future is always better. There is an opportunity now and in the future. So there is always a need for you to let go of what happened to you in the past and look forward to a better future, which is the real deal. And this should bring healing to your mind.

Learn and get knowledge about new ways of getting healing: There're several ways of getting healing. What you ought to do is be open to these new and better ways. A closed mind is a closed destiny, so learn new ways of receiving healing. There are so many people in the world today who are the cause of their own problems. They have refused to listen and accept new ways of doing things, and this has hindered their progress. For example, Buddhism is one of the most potent religions with a tradition of directly dealing with any individual who intends to gain enlightenment and knowledge about the new ways of mindfulness. Buddhism helps you to receive healing, especially with the teachings and tenets that have been modernized to help the mind develop into a state where it is capable of receiving freedom from pain and suffering. To this extent, the Buddhist has an amazing awakening knowledge about the realities of life, and how life can be lived. We can actually defeat pain and suffering, which is an inevitability in the lives of humans by following a path that will enable us to achieve that successful ending of suffering. This is one of the major causes of pain and suffering in people who actually need healing.

Open-mindedness: For you to receive healing, you need to open up your mind and be ready to receive it. People in today's world have problems not because there are no solutions but because they are unable to open up their minds and accept the healing that they truly deserve. If you are really in need of healing and you want it for yourself, you need to follow the steps explained herein, and you will be healed completely.

Spreading Peace & Loving Kindness: To spread peace and loving-kindness in the world is easy and, at the same time, difficult depending on the mindset of the individual. To preach and deliver peace to others, you need to be peaceful yourself. So the question is, are you at peace with yourself? You cannot give what you do not have, and this forms the basis of giving and receiving. Giving peace to other people has a starting point, and it begins in an individual's willingness to be open and live a peaceful life. Several people in the world today do not have peace and cannot give peace. But peace can be given by an individual, and he is capable of touching and changing lives if he is well enlightened to influence people. Peaceful living is when you are able to become a third party in a conflict situation. You are the peacemaker, you are a lover of peace, and people can trust your judgment on conflicts; that you will be able to deliver a peaceful resolution during the time of crisis or conflict.

Peaceful Protest: Sometimes in governance, there are certain decisions of the government that can be unpleasant for the masses. In these circumstances, there are protests against unpalatable decisions that tend to affect the masses, especially those that have to do with suffering. In some regions of the world, we have seen how people can take to violence if they are unable to accept what the government plans or implements against them in terms of the policy. This can be seen as an anti-people policy. In such circumstances, we usually experience what is referred to as protest or industrial action, which occasions strike. Union leaders can instigate a reasonable cause to embark on strike or industrial actions against policies that affect them. In cases like this, we can see people who understand what it means to embark on a peaceful protest without having to involve violence in the process; it's one of the highlights of living and spreading peace. If you find yourself in any organization that seems dissatisfied with policies that affect them negatively, it is your duty as a peace-loving citizen of such a country to embark to support a peaceful resolution of crises. Or at least, if it seems too likely to become violent, advocate a peaceful process or protest to resolve the crisis. This is one of the ways of spreading peace.

Live a life of Generosity: Living a life of generosity doesn't mean you need to have before you give. Generosity is not only dependent on material gifts. What you can give to people may be something worth more than material gifts. A person may need love. There are so many people who are in need of good advice, and others who need a shoulder to lean on. We have people in the world who really need people they can say hi to, people they can confide in, people they can talk to. You can reach out to that person. It doesn't necessarily mean you have to reach everyone, but the change and giving in generosity can be achieved if you are able to make a move. There are various movements and religions in the world which began with one person. And today, we have millions of people who have been touched by such religions;

Buddhism is one of them. The practice started with one man, the Buddha, and today we have over 400 million Buddhist followers. Be generous in your gifts and talents. If you have a talent or are blessed with a special gift that can help you touch and change lives, do it. And in so doing, you will be able to make a change and transformation through your generous gift to mankind.

Share what you have with others: The more you give to others, the more you will receive. This is great teaching which has been on for thousands of years. There is more joy in giving than in receiving. The most successful people in the world are not those who have taken pleasure in stolen wealth or become rich by inflicting pain on other people. Rather, the most successful people in the world today are people who have knowledge of the teaching of the art of giving. A person who gives is the person who gets the blessing. That is just one of the basic teachings of life. Successful people are able to cultivate the habit of giving back to the society what the society has blessed them with. I wouldn't want to mention names, but I know you are aware of many foundations and charity organizations in the world today. Some are very popular, and some are not so popular. Nonetheless, these organizations have been able to touch lives and contributed immensely to the solving of various human problems. Problems such as providing help to the needy, food for orphanages, relief materials during crisis or conflicts, etc. This is how you can perform acts of giving and kindness to people around you. You can partner with or set up NGO's that can work towards spreading love and kindness to people who are in need, or you can just start a personal course which can lead to a great change.

Show tolerance to people irrespective of age, culture, and race: One of the greatest problems the world has ever faced is racism and intolerance for people of different races and origins. When you have the tendency to show preference and segregation among people, and if you have a prejudicial notion about people, it is a sign that you are not creating a better world. Rather, you are simply making non-peaceful co-existence among people. Learn to show tolerance to people and accept them the way they are. Don't ever think you are any better than other people because all people came from one source. So it is not healthy to stigmatize or segregate people based on color, race, or religion.

Be charitable: One of the best ways you can spread kindness to people is to become charitable. Be charitable and contribute to helping people so that they can live a normal life. There are people who need food, children without parents, no education, and no means of livelihood. Some of these children or young persons get exposed to life on the street. Very few usually escape, but so many have lost their lives on the street struggling to survive. You can reach out to these people and help them to become better citizens.

Visit the sick in hospitals: Lots of people are sick in hospitals. You can visit them and do the little you can to give a helping hand. If you chose to pay the medical bill of one person, you would have done very well by touching the life of that person. You don't have to help the whole world, but you can start by helping someone out of a desperate situation in the hospital.

Do free Empowerment: One of the best ways to really show kindness to people is to empower them with skills. This is a fact because; the best way to help a person is not when you are able to give material gifts. If you give a fish to a person, he will come back the next day to ask for another fish. So why not teach a man how to fish, and he will become the fisherman who will learn how to catch fish and also teach others? That is how life ought to be. Life is about learning and empowering people by teaching them the right path to achieve success and survive. Many people in the world today lack the basic skills and knowledge to survive. To feed and live a normal life becomes a problem when there is no basic training. So you can do something about that, especially if you are an expert, and you know how to train people and educate them in a particular skill. You can share it with people who need help, and you would have succeeded in saving their future. Helping people is one of the ways of making them become peaceful, and that way, you have spread love and kindness through your own efforts.

CHAPTER 2

What is Buddhism?

Buddhism is an ancient religion that was started by Buddha, and it is a spiritual tradition that began over two thousand, six hundred years ago in Nepal. It was started by a certain young man who meditated under a Bodhi tree and got enlightenment. This led to the laying of the foundation of the spiritual tradition of Buddhism.

Origins of Buddhism

Basically, Buddhism is a religion that bears its roots in India, a country located on the Asian continent. The religion was founded on the basic teachings of a man who went on meditating. He happens to be a Buddha who is a person that practices the art of teaching people on spirituality. He bears this title "Buddha," which is drawn from the belief that such a person is the "awakened one." This name was coined around the 5th BCE century following the event that took place.

The early description given to Buddha was that his biological name or real name was "Siddhartha

Gautama." However, the descriptions of the Buddha's lifestyle, as written by many authors have been inconsistent. Meanwhile, his background as Buddha is difficult to trace. However, the early documentations on his background depicted Gautama Siddhartha to have been born in Lumbini and brought up in Ganges Plain, in Nepal, along the Indian border. The Buddha was said to have spent his life in what is now referred to as the Bihar in modern-day India and in parts of Uttar as well. There are, however, disputes about his royalty status because early writers claimed he came from a royal family. However, scholars claim that rather, he was from a Shakya community.

The Shakya community was one that was ruled by a small, rich family or republic-like council that based its leadership on seniority, but the ranking wasn't supreme. The life and times of Buddha from a historical perspective have been inconsistent because the authors' works gave divergent views about Buddha. This is not to say that everything about Buddha wasn't a fact. In every religion, there is always some truth in its teaching, which Buddha has been able to thrive with over 400 million followers around the world.

The Story of Siddhārtha Gautama

Buddha was a mortal man and not a god. He was referred to as Siddhārtha Gautama by name. He saw the selfishness, violence, and sadness exhibited by a man in his environment. Because this often led to human suffering, he made his determination to find a solution to end the various suffering of human beings. He went on to study great spiritualists, ascetics, gurus, sages, etc. He further went on to exclude himself from the public and sat under a Bodhi tree. And with a deep meditation practice that took place for about 49 days, he gained great enlightenment and was willing to share his knowledge and newly learned spiritual orientation.

Some writers also claimed that Buddha was given birth to and named Siddhartha Gautama around two thousand six hundred years ago; he was said to be a prince of the monastic order in the Sakya clan in Nepal. Because he wrote two hundred and twenty-seven rules for the monks and three hundred and eleven rules for monks and nuns respectively, these rules were to be followed and guide their activities. His death was known as parinivana, and he also suggested that there can be changes to the rules he created.

Over the course of time, there was disagreement between the brotherhood of the Buddha. This gave birth to sectionalism and separation, which created different sects that eventually emerged among the monks. It was clear there was a divide. Some sects emerged and referred to themselves as the Mahayana sect and Hinayana sect. These were the two major sects that emerged, and the Mahayana sect referred to themselves as the greater vehicle while they referred to the Hinayana sect as the lesser sect or conservatives. Among the remaining Hinayana sect in the modern day is the Theravada sect. Many developments have occurred throughout the years thereafter.

For over two thousand six hundred years, Buddhism as a religion has evolved and is the major source of inspiration responsible for successful modern-day civilization. It became the source of inspiration and major breakthrough in achievements in the lives of millions of people around the world. People from different backgrounds and cultures are now students of Buddha teachings and are following and learning from what Buddhism has to offer.

Buddhism 101

Buddhism was founded many years ago and has been able to inspire millions of people around the world with the ability to generate peaceful teachings that emanate, radiate, and touch lives. Buddhism 101 teachings are about the explanation of the central concepts behind the successful practice of Buddhism in modern-day society. These are applicable and practicable in modern times while providing information that is based on mindfulness, karma, the middle way, the four noble truths, and much more. This teaching constitutes what is referred to as Buddhism 101.

They are what guide you to understand the basic operations or principles of the Buddhism religion. Buddhism helps people who are interested in teaching and religion to get to understand what life is all about and how to follow the Buddhist way of getting enlightenment. The philosophy behind the study of Buddhism and becoming a practitioner will help you to live as an enlightened individual in the world. Irrespective of color, tribe, or race, you can explore the Buddhism 101.

The Basics of Buddhism

One of the most interesting things about Buddhism is its basic teachings. These dwell on doctrines that started from the early days, when Buddhism was established and which are still prevalent in the modern era of Buddhism practice. It is made up of the four noble truths which are very obvious in the world today. The basic teachings referred to as the four noble truths are:

1. "Dukkha" meaning the existence of suffering and which further stresses that.

2. Suffering has a cause, called craving and attachment, referred to as "Trishna."

3. Cessation of suffering is referred to as "nirvana," and there is also a way to the stopping of suffering which is further categorized into.

4. The right resolve, right action, right livelihood, right mindfulness, right effort, right concentration, right views, and right speech.

It is basically based on the relationships and realities that Buddhism proposes in its concept and precept. It is not based on substance or deity or an entity that exists somewhere. Its basic teaching is based on what is realistic and obtainable and also can be practiced.

The basics of Buddhism are also propounded into five wholesome teachings, which are purely based on experience constituting the "skandhas." They form the "Rupa" which is known as material existence. The next in the compilation are the four basics, which are sensations known as "Vedana." The other that follows is what is referred to as the concept of perceptions known as "Samina." There are also the psychic constructs commonly referred to as the "samskara," the consciousness aspect is known as the "Vijnana," and all these are summed up as the psychological process.

The most central teaching is based on non-self "anatman" which stipulates in 5 compilations that there is no independent existence, self-immunity, or soul.

The school teaches that every (circumstance) or phenomenon takes place for the purpose of a course and conditions. In so doing, they will definitely be subjected to an ending or cessation.

It also teaches that there is some form of casual occurrence which takes place. They are summed up in a 12-group chain called "Pratityasamutpada" and are dependent on the origin. This group of 12 chains is known to be responsible for these characteristics exhibited by individuals; predisposition, consciousness, ignorance, the senses, the name form, cravings, contact, birth, gasping, aging old and death, more ignorance.

These teachings revolve around an individual's birth, destiny, and death and returning to life to continue, depending on where such individual had ended. The term "continual circle of an individual" is a common term in Buddhism. Moral precepts were the basic foundation of Buddhism from inception until a deeper study based on meditation and enlightenment was further revealed.

The regulation of monastic life was based on non-participation in vices that were alien to monastic life, including stealing and immorality. Non-participation in entertainment, especially secular entertainment, refraining from viewing secular entertainment, avoiding ornaments and bodily adornment, etc. were prioritized in the practice of Buddhism.

5 Steps to Start Buddhist Meditation

There are basically five steps to start meditation. These steps, when carefully followed, will yield results and you will be amazed by the effects viz-a-viz:

Self-Awareness: In the practice of Buddhism, awareness does not refer to the usual awareness that a layman would describe or express according to his knowledge. To people generally, awareness, in ordinary words, is to be informed or know what is going on around you. But in Buddhism, the first thing you need to have to start your meditation is awareness. In the real sense, in a Buddhist expression or in Buddhism, awareness simply means "awakening of oneself." Simply put, it is to be "awake" or being awakened to what you have around you. This includes having the sense of feeling, smell, colors of objects, the material things around you, knowing or being knowledgeable of what is going on around you, but yet refusing to be pulled or distracted by them. The state of mind is always in the present pristine state. When you are able to command the present and don't allow yourself to be distracted by what is going on around you, that means that you have started your first step to meditation in Buddhism. Applying this to your daily life will help you to be less distracted by worries or criticism, and you can make things better if you follow the practice.

A lot of hardship can come from your family, wants, needs, and desires. Friends can cause you problems, enemies may be against you, and they want you to fail. Also, there can be injustice around you; but you need to free yourself from these problems by starting meditation. Buddha started by meditation to change his present and future. You cannot change your past, but you can influence your future to suit yourself if you are suffering today. Buddha started with the awareness of his mind, his body, and the reality about things around him.

Thinking: Thinking here is based on what we experience in relation to just seeing, touching, and tasting. For example, we are staying with the body while doing the job, without thinking about the job, sticking to the process, so that the action is in the body experience. The functioning doesn't have to come from the head, only allowing the action to take place naturally in the body. In this instance, it is void of thoughts or thinking; it is beyond thinking and is usually an unlettered experience. The process is void of any other addition to it. Thinking only makes the mind more confused, so while you experience what goes on around you, do not allow the thinking or feeling or smell, etc. of those things to distract you.

Thinking is actually good for some people, no doubt. Thinking makes them plan or arrange appointments or think of doing things. This is not the type of thinking that works in Buddhism. The successful kind of thinking in Buddhism is the one that has to come from the inner mind. The one that has to do with inspiration, detaching yourself from what is around you and thoughtfulness that radiates inwards is exactly what we are talking about.

Meditation: Meditation that has to do with the awakening of the mind should be void of sleep. Meditation that leads to sleeping off is not Buddhism. Complete enlightenment is derived through meditation from a sitting position void of distraction. Meditation that awakens the reality of the moment suffices as the real act of Buddhism compared to sleeping and dreaming. Meditation cures ignorance; it is great medicine for being ignorant because, through meditation, the individual is awakened. It awakens the reality of life and exposes a person just like an individual standing in front of a mirror exposes himself to the way he is, void of any hidden secret. The mysteries of life can be seen through meditation, which opens up the depth of great awareness in the reality of life that exists in our daily activity.

Meditation by sitting or Sitting Meditation: This process involves finding a quiet place to carry out meditation where you are free from interruption from anyone or anything. It can usually be carried out in a noiseless room; specifically, it can be done in a little corner of the room. This particular activity involves the voiding of every distraction that can come from your spouse or children, including telephone calls or text messages, no matter what they are. Make it clear to members of your family that you should not be disturbed at this point in time. If you allow disturbance, the whole process will not be effective, and you will not get a good result out of it. In modern times, finding a quiet place outside your room may be difficult, especially in the urban city, which is usually noisy. So create a space in your room and make the room sealed from distraction. Take note that your family may see your decision as awkward and selfish, but let them understand that you deserve some level of privacy, which ought to be respected. If others want to learn or participate in the process, it's acceptable to give them the opportunity too. This means meditation can also be done in groups with a full understanding of the teaching.

Sitting Positions: The sitting positions are easy, especially for young people, but maybe difficult for adults. The traditional position is the lotus posture, which requires some effort to start with and it is the most appealing position.

Half Lotus position: The half-lotus position is another positioning that can be difficult for adults to attain and which is also necessary and required in the Buddhist position for meditation.

Crossed Leg Posture: The crossed leg posture helps to make the meditation and adjustment a lot easier; of the three ways of positioning for meditation, crossed leg posture happens to be the choice of most Buddhist practitioners.

Kneeling: Some people may prefer to kneel, this is also acceptable especially if the crossed leg posture happens to be difficult. Kneeling can also be enhanced with the aid of materials like a cushion or stool designed for the purpose of kneeling.

Sitting on a Chair: It is also acceptable for you to sit on a chair if possible because when you meditate, it should be out of being comfortable from any distractions around you. It is advisable to practice the various positions in a sequence so you can find the best position that will fit or that you are comfortable with.

The positioning of Hands and Eyes: Here, you will need to open your eyes and look down at the floor and your feet without placing your attention or focus on any other thing. The position of the arms should be inwards, placing your palm on top of the other palm of your hands, not holding on tight but in a loose manner.

Duration of the Meditation: It is advisable to start with a short duration like ten minutes, which can be gradually increased from ten to fifteen and to twenty minutes in subsequent days. Follow these steps to get the right duration, and do not start thinking about how long it will take you to complete the process. Normally, it is not the duration that really matters but the quality of it. So make sure you get the very best out of your time taken to meditate. The sitting position should be void of the endurance of pain. Rather it should be done with great enthusiasm. Otherwise, it will become worthless when you feel pained, and you seem to be agonizing rather than embracing the situation.

When to Meditate: The best time to meditate may not usually be fixed, but it is advisable to do your meditation when the environment is void of distraction. Some Buddhist practitioners suggest early in the morning, but this depends on the circumstances. It is ideal, however, to do your mediation in the middle of the afternoon when, maybe your kids have gone to school, or late at night when every person around you is asleep. Or anytime there will be silence, you can do your meditation—you will have to figure it out yourself. You can decide to meditate when the time is right and the number of times depends on you. You can decide to meditate more than once or twice a day; it all depends on your preference.

Starting: once you have started, you can begin taking a position with overlapping palms on your laps. You have prepared your mind towards the course, and there is no looking back and, of course, no distraction.

Counting Your Breaths: Counting your breaths is done gradually, and ten successive breaths are usually counted. If there is a loss of count, you will have to start all over again. Inhaling and exhaling should be done in a gradual process, taking your mind off it during the exercise. If there is wandering away of the mind from the focus, you will need to start all over again. The main purpose of the exercise is to bring you into reality. The process is also to seek the discovery of self and how the mind works. This process will awaken you to the realities. Don't see it as a moment of depression, and do not begin to fill disinterested in what you are doing. Always try to bring your mind back into the exercise even if your concentration is not sufficient, repeated practice will get you going. Exercise patience in carrying on the activity. The secret behind the counting of breaths is that it helps in the concentration of the mind and removing it from all forms of worry and distraction. It enables you to be in the reality and moment of the practice.

Meditation helps to bring you into the real issues and aids the bringing of solutions to problems with the new awakening. It also develops positivism and clears all negative thoughts.

While this takes place, there is the development of a high level of concentration, which varies from one individual to another. In some persons, it may be instant. However, it may take a little while like weeks or months in some people, and this varies. So, yours may be different from another person.

Non-Attachment: let your mind be focused on the moment, don't get involved in responding to what happens around you. Don't involve yourself in thinking of who is watching or what is passing by. Rather, focus on the fulfillment of the function of what you are doing. If you get distracted, you will not be free, and it will affect your meditation. When you free yourself from the pleasurable things of life, you will get to the realm of happiness, and the freedom of the mind opens up new discoveries.

A Typical Day

Doing your meditation a daily routine or habit is one of the significant processes that lead to the total transformation of the individual. It means, to become successful, you have to create your personal daily mindfulness, and if you do, you are already on the path of Buddhism experience. It has to do with making use of your daily behavioral tendencies in which you will be able to manage a particular set of schedules. This implies that you have to become resolute in taking action. Not just designing a schedule that you will find difficult to follow up, but a mindset of taking action on such a schedule of activities.

Often, human beings tend to take preference for what is easier to do than what is not easy to do. Waking up in the morning and preparing for work may not be easy for some people, but it becomes easy when it becomes a daily routine. That is the essence of a schedule because you will become used to it. Even if it is difficult, it becomes easy because you do it regularly. Another face to it is that at least when things are easier, we tend to show preference to do it more often and better. So, the six steps to daily meditation are as follows:

- **Make a decision to maintain a particular schedule of meditation that will be consistent:** To put up a meditation session; you should make efforts to schedule a time for meditation. If you don't fix a time, you will keep on procrastinating it and won't be able to stick to a particular time. That's the first step in the right direction; when you schedule a time for your meditation and also stick to it consistently. After your meditation, make sure you keep an appointment for the next day. This way, you will know and have it at the back of your mind. It may not be easy at first, but when you are consistent with it, you will definitely get used to it; your mind will become focused on a schedule that you get accustomed to.

  Meditating in the morning when you wake up is very beneficial and can help you start that way before you decide to pick a time. Make sure you don't miss your daily meditation, no excuses. In the event something comes up to interrupt your schedule for a day, you can reschedule the meditation for that day. Make sure you carry it out without allowing a day to pass without doing your meditation.

- **Form a dedicated space for Meditation:** Create a space that will enable you to perform your meditation; this should be a noiseless and less distraction environment which is suited for performing meditation. Get anything that will disrupt your sitting position out of the place of your meditation. Don't allow distraction items like television, radio, computers, windows, and any other items that can cause distraction in the space. The purpose of the least resistance is to make sure we discover our tendencies, not just the distraction. Due to human tendency, it is possible to put on your smartphone, or start browsing on your computer or be tempted to put on your television. These items offer the least resistance, and this is going to take away the main focus of your meditation.

- **Mindfulness of breath:** Start practicing your mindfulness of breath while keeping it simple. I have explained about breathing above. It helps to start your meditation on the right path by calming your mind and gradually building up the mindfulness around your meditation. Secondly, it makes things easy for you, where your mind can move into the moment and reality. Thirdly, it enables the expansion of your Buddhism practice beyond your sitting position and enables you to bring meditation into your daily life.

- **The One-Minute Jump Start technique:** You start by meditating for one minute. While you monitor your progress, visualize if you experience any mental push. Try sitting down for ten seconds and continue for the first week until you get used to it. This process is to enable you to get used to meditation. When this is done in the first week through the second week, you are already on your way to making meditating a daily routine.

- **Mindfulness practice in daily activity aside sitting meditation:** Practicing mindfulness in your daily activities or lifestyle is a way of helping you during meditation; mindfulness doesn't have to be practiced only when you are meditating alone. You can practice mindfulness, as explained in this book earlier throughout your daily life. This will enable you to adjust and improve your meditation. There are various ways you can do daily life practice of meditation, such as when you are driving, walking, or eating. All you do at these moments is to practice mindfulness, and it will help improve your meditation process.

CHAPTER 3

The Teaching of Buddhism

The teaching of Buddhism is to enable the individual, irrespective of class, gender, race, or color, to arrive at a path of perfect enlightenment. This is the ultimate goal, which will be attained when followed with due diligence. The teachings based on the path of arriving at perfect enlightenment are referred to as Dharma, which in ordinary meaning is known as "the nature of all things." Or it can also be known as the "truth in the existence of things." The Buddha teaching can be categorized into seven subtopics which are:

1. The Noble Eightfold Path

2. The path to perfect enlightenment (Dharma)

3. Suffering and Neurosis

4. Non-self

5. Sutras

6. Karma and

7. Reincarnation

The Noble Eightfold Path

The Noble eightfold path is teaching that implies the path to end all suffering because it prevents two extremes of sensitive indulgence and mortification of self. It is based on when the body is in a state of comfort and not overindulge. Thereby the mind is at the clarity and has the energy to meditate inwardly and deeply to uncover the truth. The noble eightfold is made of mindful cultivation of virtue, wisdom, and meditation. The Noble Eightfold paths are:

- The Right Understanding
- The Right Thought
- The Right Speech
- The Right Action
- The Right Livelihood
- The Right Effort
- The Right Mindfulness and
- The Right Concentration

The training in virtue and/or morality comprises "the right speech, the right livelihood, and the right action."

The Buddhism practice is engulfed in the practice of 5 major precepts which the tradition and religion teach as:

1. Refraining from deliberate causing of the death of any being that is living and has life.

2. Refraining from the deliberate taking for one's own property belonging to another person.

3. Sexual immorality or misconduct, especially adultery.

4. Breaking promises and lying.

5. Drug abuse and alcoholism can cause a lack of mindfulness.

The mindfulness, the right effort, and the right concentration are regarded in the practice of meditation. It is the path that purifies the mind via the experience of a blissful status of internal firmness. It makes provision for the empowerment of the mind to go into the deeper meaning of life via a great moment of enlightened insight.

The Right Thought and the Right Understanding are what make up the revelation of the wisdom of Buddhism, which is always viewed as the ending of all suffering. Also, it is usually said to cause the great transformation of an individual. This is done by producing an unfettered conducive mind and unstirred passion. The person is transformed, and the level of understanding transcends beyond the ordinary man.

The Buddhism practice of this virtue is postulated from the fact that without the perfection of the practice of virtue, it becomes impossible to carry out a perfect meditation. Thus, such an individual will be unable to get the enlightenment and wisdom of Buddhism. The path of Buddhism is a process that brings about gradual development. It is a gradual process comprising the practice of virtue, wisdom, and meditation, as stipulated by the Noble Eightfold Path, which causes or leads to the liberation and happiness in an individual.

Dharma - The Path to Perfect Enlightenment

The word "Dharma" has been used in some religions such as Hinduism, Jainism, etc., and may confer a different meaning in different religions. However, in Buddhism, it means cosmic law and order, which is also applied to the teaching of Buddha. The term is also used in Buddhist philosophy to describe phenomena. The term has evolved to be applied for different usage over the years, such as being postulated as the doctrine that teaches purification and transformation of human beings.

Suffering and Neurosis

The literal meaning of suffering is bearing pain, loss, or inconvenience. When pain is endured, or a distress situation or injury is incurred by an individual, the term suffering applies; or when a person is in sorrow, pain, or grief. But in Buddhism, the Buddhist recognizes the existence of suffering that is based on a cause. And that such suffering for a cause definitely has an ending. Also, there is something that will bring it to an end. Buddhists teach that ignorance and desires are at the root of suffering. Desires in the parlance of Buddhism mean the urge for pleasure in materialism and immorality, which are desires that cannot be satisfied as long as human beings are concerned.

Neurosis is a term that is associated with a person experiencing emotional pain or unconscious distress, which can be seen in some form of illness like mental disorders. The tendencies of neurotic illnesses vary in the degree of affliction, which can be chronic and manifest in the person. Problems like anxiety, obsession, phobia, and disorders are typical examples.

In Buddhism, it is a common phenomenon that you might experience some form of over activeness or noticing changes in behavioral patterns. Note that this is not a Neurotic problem but simply because you're getting deeper into enlightenment.

What Is Non-Self?

Non-self in Buddhism simply means substance-less, and the term is often referred to as Sanskrit Anatman. The teaching on non-self is that in every human, there is no permanent nature or substance that can be referred to as a soul that the human body embodies in an enclave. The teaching is a deviation from the Hindu belief in Atman, which means "the self."

What Are the Sutras?

The meaning of sutras in Buddhism is a set of scriptures (conical) that are known as records of the oral doctrines and teachings or tradition of Gautama Buddha. They are very detailed scriptures that have sometimes been compiled. Found repeatedly in the scripts are words that further emphasize the teachings; it is rooted in spoken words. Other religions, like Hinduism, also recognize and use sutras.

What Is Karma?

Karma in Buddhism simply means *'action.'* The term is usually referred and linked to "the law of Karma." The implication of this is that for every action we take, there are consequences of such actions that we cannot escape. The teaching on this is that there are certain deeds, speeches, or mindful actions that lead to the harming of oneself or others. These actions are referred to as bad or unwholesome karma. The teachings identify hatred, greed, and wickedness to be linked to getting returns or consequences as the law of karma demands.

Since harmful acts will end up giving an individual a resultant painful effect, then Buddhism advises individuals to desist from such bad actions. Alternatively, teaching in Buddhism also recognizes positive Karma, which is based on actions of generosity, kindness, wisdom, and compassion. The Buddhist encourages people to perform such actions because they bring good results and are therefore referred to as good or wholesome karma. They bring happy ending results.

When a person is affected in life, when he has a misfortune, the teaching is that you cannot blame someone else for such misfortune. Rather, look inwards, it's probably something bad you did in the past that is affecting you, and you are getting bad results now. But when something good happens to you, it's a result of the good karma you did in the past, and you are getting good results accordingly. The teaching encourages the performance of good deeds so that you will always get good karma in the future. The teaching on Buddhism is that there is no superior or divine being that is responsible for the karma that happens to an individual, either good or bad. And such consequences are never controlled by a divine being. The proposition is also emphasized by reaping what you sow. Hence the Buddhist teaches the performance of good deeds to get good karma and not bad deeds.

However, the teaching on karma also stipulates that bad karma can be mitigated by doing more good karma. If there is pending bad karma, it will be reduced. If there is a lot of bad karma, the more one is required to do more good karma to reduce the painful results. Bad deeds are often seen as bad habits that should be avoided. Moral practices in our contemporary society are the impact that the law of karma has had on the lives of millions of people around the world.

What Is Reincarnation?

The reincarnation teaching in Buddhism is all about bringing to memory the past life an individual lived and bringing it into the realms of meditation. The remembrance of the past life established the rebirths which direct the life of the person in a meaningful or purposeful perspective. This enables a better understanding of the framework of the law of Karma. Normally it takes some time for karma to emerge.

Therefore, reincarnation gives a good exhibition to the notable inequalities of the birth of an individual. Some are born into abject poverty while some are born into wealthy families; some come into the world with deformity while some come into the world with full form void of deformity. These are not, however, proof of bad karma but the understanding that we should be generous to avert bad karma.

The rebirth of an individual is not based only on the present human world. Buddhism teaches that the realms of men or humans are more than just one. There are separate realms that are high, and there are realms that are higher in perspective. There are animal realms, and there are realms belonging to spirits. Buddhism teaches that humans can transcend to any of these realms and can even condescend to human life from any of these realms. The teachings state that many people in the world today came from different realms believed to exist in Buddhism.

The substantive issue involved in this teaching is that there should be regard for living beings because we all came from any of these realms, and we will be going back to any of the realms. That process constitutes the reincarnation in Buddhism, and there is an understanding of a connection with these realms.

What Is the Abhidharma?

Abhidharma is generally referred to in Buddhism as the ancient 3rd century BCE Buddhist scripts that consist of well-informed reworking of the doctrinal materials contained in the Buddhist sutra. It was developed from the scattered teachings of Buddha during this era and was compiled to the scriptures concerning conscious thoughts based on exposing and developing conscious thoughtfulness.

What Is Yoga?

Yoga is a form of body and mind practice that has to do with meditation and combining various methods of positioning. It has been in existence for the past five thousand years, and its philosophy bears its origin from India. Yoga combines the features of meditation, breathing techniques, and physical positioning to enhance relaxation. Yoga has become well known all over the world because it is developed and practiced based on physical exercise. This helps in improving and controlling the body and mind to enhance the wellness of an individual or practitioner of yoga. Yoga, therefore, is a form of meditation and exercise in a general perspective. But in relation to Buddhism, Yoga is aimed towards the enlightenment of the individual through meditation, which is also yoga. The combination of yoga and Buddhist meditation helps to guard the fluctuations of the mind. This helps to keep the oneness of the mind and body which the Buddhist commonly refers to as emptiness.

Postures of Buddha

In Buddhism, there are about four suitable postures that depend and can be practiced by an individual, depending on his preference. They are the standing posture, the sitting posture, the reclining posture, and the walking posture.

5 Zen Buddhism Teachings

The teachings of Zen Buddhism, classified into 5, which can be practiced on a daily basis in modern times, are summarized as follows:

1. **Meditation technique:** It is based on individual preference by finding the right technique that suits you. Also, it will enable you to get the required result and aims of meditation.
2. **Enjoying the Moment:** Each moment of your day should be lived consciously without being afraid or burdened. You should live each moment enjoying it. It's not as if you will not have difficult moments, but just keep it simple and enjoy it.
3. **Being Happy:** Staying happy is finding the need to be happy within yourself. Happiness is not found outside. Your job, your business, or your relationship may give you some level of happiness, but you may not have the power to control happiness from the outside. You can only control happiness from the inside. You stay happy because you are happy and not because you get the influence from outside.
4. **Stay Focused:** To focus means you are following through all the activities such as the routine, ritual, and habits that support the Zen

way of Buddhism. You don't necessarily have to be a Zen monk, but you can stay focused on the habits to get results.

5. **Be Alive:** The Zen way of living means that you should be alive. You are not living in anticipation of what will happen or in panic. Instead, you live a normal simple life, void of a rush to get wants or needs. Living a life helping people and deriving happiness in such is being alive the Zen way.

CHAPTER 4

Buddhism Numbers 3

The use of numbering is a unique system in the history of Buddhism literature. It shows the cultural background in India and some other parts of Asia, where Buddhism gained development. This system of numbering gave taxonomies to different enlightenment.

The 3 Jewels of Refuge

The three jewels of Refuge in the Buddhism tradition are "the completely enlightened one," known as "The Buddha." The second is "the Teachings given by the Buddha," which is known as "the Dharma." The third is "Buddhism," which is the monastic order that practices the Dharma known as the Sangha.

The 3 Higher Trainings

Buddhism recognizes three higher trainings which are:

1) **Higher Virtue Training**
   This aspect has to do with great virtue, which is based on the higher morality standard with

awesome simplicity suitable for good behavioral traits. Such that the behavior will conform with the universally accepted standards, which cause no distress for another person or the person involved. This virtue is contained in the five moral precepts or eight folds of the Buddhism teachings. It is also referenced in the 227 rules. To live out these teachings, one must understand and practice them through conduct by way of body language, speech, and general conduct aimed at bringing peace to all living bodies. It also includes the total showing and practicing of convenience in a relationship. And freedom from unpalatable effects at the simplest level of living in the world. These should transcend selfish interest. It is connected to members of a particular social group with involvements in the properties of a group, which are a very important aspect of human lives.

2) **The Higher Mind Training**

   The higher mind training is one of the three higher trainings that have to do with the concentration level of the mind, otherwise known as the "Samadhi." This comprises the constraining of the mind to maintain the condition that is most convenient to receive success in whatever the person wishes to achieve. You might ask, what is the meaning of concentration in Buddhism? Obviously, people always understand concentration to mean a completely steady mind. As steady and unmoving as an unmovable log of wood. However, these two behaviors, being steady and unmovable, do not really define concentration. The basis of these words was an utterance of the Buddha. Buddha described a concentrated mind as the mind that is fit for work, referred to as the 'Kammaniya.' This is the best suitable condition for doing a job. A mind that is "fit for work" is the best way to describe what it means to have a concentrated mind.

3) **The Higher Wisdom Training**

The higher wisdom training (Panna) is teaching that dwells on insight. This is a practice and drilling that gives birth to the full measure of proper knowledge, comprehension, or understanding the true nature of many or all things. Naturally, we are incapable of knowing any living being or anything by its true nature. Often, we only do things or act according to our own ideas. Or we are used to following popular opinion about something, and in so doing, what we normally see is not the truth. Based on this reality, the Buddhist practice includes the insightful training of the mind to attain wisdom, which is the last aspect of the three-fold training of the mind in order to gain understanding and insight into the true nature of all things.

The 3 Universal Truths

In Buddhism, there are basically three universal truths, and they are:

1) Nothing Is Lost to the Universe

The truth and reality are that nothing is lost in the universe. The transformation of matter into energy and from energy into matter is something that takes place in a circle of life according to Buddhist teaching. For instance, a dead leaf returns to the soil. A fruit, when ripe, falls back to the soil. The seed sprouts and it becomes a new plant, and this life cycle continues. The old solar systems disappear and turn into cosmic dust or rays. People are born of their parents, and our children are our offspring, all these continue in life cycles.

All living beings are the same as plants, like other people, as trees, as the rain that falls. All are life cycles; we are part of the system that surrounds us, and we constitute the same things that we see. If we damage anything around us, we are destroying ourselves. If we cheat others or anything, we are equally cheating ourselves. Because of the knowledge and understanding of these basic teachings and truths, the Buddha and his followers do not kill other animals.

2) Everything Changes

This teaching is a universal truth postulated by Buddha that in this world, everything is constantly changing. Life can be compared to a river flowing and always changing. Sometimes the speed of flow may be slow, and sometimes it can be fast. Sometimes it can be smooth and gentle, depending on the location and nature. Sometimes rivers are found within rocky environments. This implies that we can presume or think that we are always safe, but unfortunately, we are not always safe. Such is life and the teachings in Buddhism.

Our ideas about life also continue to change, but the basic truth will always remain. The kind of life that dominated the earth thousands of years ago is not what we have now. Once upon a time, we had bigger or larger animals and beasts such as dinosaurs and others. Archaeology has discovered the debris of these animals, and since they have gone into extinction, does this mean that life did not continue? Of course not, life went on to produce new forms of animals which we have to this day. Things continue to change and take different forms.

3) Law of Cause and Effect

Buddha teaches that there are changes in the world because of the law of cause and effect. This principle is what is also observed in the teaching of modern science. Furthermore, this goes forth to prove that Buddhism and science are somewhat similar in finding out realities about living and non-living things.

The teaching, according to the law of Karma, is also based on the law of cause and effect. It teaches that nothing ever happens to an individual unless the individual deserves it. It teaches that an individual receives exactly what he earns, whether bad or good. We are what we are now because of what we did in the past. Our actions and thoughts will determine the nature of life that we are going to have. If we do bad things, in the future, bad things happen to us. If we do good, the same way good things will happen to us in the future. Likewise, every moment we live our lives, we create karma by the words we say or through the things we do and/or think. If we have knowledge of these teachings, we will not have to be afraid of Karma, but we will be friends of karma. With it, we can create a bright future for ourselves and our generations unborn. This is the teaching of Buddhism.

The 3 Poisons

Buddhism teaches about three forms of poisons. The poisons are thought to be responsible for the keeping of sentient beings locked up in the samsara. They are aversion, attachment, and ignorance. These characteristics take their root in the Kleshas category.

The Different Schools of Buddhism

Theravada is one of the schools reserved for the elders, and it is the oldest school in Buddhism. The school is responsible for the preservation of the traditions of Gautama Buddha (their version) of the teaching, which is availed as the Pali Canon. It is the only surviving full Buddhist teachings in an Indian language that provide the sacred language from which Buddhism originated. The Theravada follows the path of conservatism in monastic discipline and doctrinal matters of Buddhism.

Mahayana

The Mahayana is one of the two main branches of schools in Buddhism and is popularly known as "the Great Vehicle." This school dwells on seeking complete enlightenment for the gratification of all sentient bodies or beings simply referred to as the Bodhisattva vehicle. Any Bodhisattva who completes the school is referred to as the completely enlightened Buddha. It teaches that enlightenment in the school can be achieved by a layperson and that it can also be attained in a lifetime. It has over 54% of membership practitioners in modern times, which is higher than the Theravada.

Vajrayana

The term Vajrayana in Buddhism is referred to as "Diamond Vehicle" or the "Thunderbolt Vehicle." This is linked to a mythical weapon often used as a ritual and called vajra. The teachings of Vajrayana are the practice that utilizes Mantras, Mudras, Dharanis, and Mandalas. They often see the existence of deities and their usage and also follow the Buddha routes to enlightenment as part of their practice. The school was founded by middle age Indian, Mahasiddhas.

Buddhist Philosophy 101

The teaching in Buddhism that has to do with the philosophy and acceptability of certain facts of life is the philosophy of the Buddhist. This includes acceptance of the fact that disease is inevitable, and that emotional pains in the life of a human being and death cannot be prevented from happening. It teaches that human sufferings are the major reasons for attachment to things that are created with form. The solution offers to cure suffering means to detach yourself from these attachments that tend to influence life. Practical means of attaining this have been stipulated in the Noble eight meditations.

The 4 Noble Truths

In Buddhism, there are four realities and truces, which are referred to as Noble Truths. These teach about human suffering and are described as:

1. **Dukkha:** This is a teaching that suffering exists in life; it is a real occurrence and is universal in nature. It teaches that with suffering, there are causes which can be illness, loss, pain, failure, and the non-permanency of the pleasures of life.

2. **The Samudaya:** The Samudaya teaches that there is a cause of suffering and that suffering is caused by attachment. It stipulated that suffering arises as a result of the desire to control and own things. The forms that this may take are when we crave after sensual pleasure, fame, and the will to avoid unpleasant feelings such as anger, jealousy, and fear.

3. **The Nirodha:** This teaching talks about the end of suffering. It suggests that attachment can be defeated or overcome, and the mind experiences total liberation, freedom, and non-attachment. The mind becomes void of

desires, and suffering ends with the last liberation of Nirvana.

4. **The Magga:** This teaching emphasizes the following and implementation or practice of the Eight-Fold Path, which is the path to accomplishing the end to suffering.

The 4 Dharma Seals

In Buddhism, Dharma Seals are four, and they can be translated and described in summary as "all compounded things are not permanent." The teachings also emphasize that emotions are suffering pain and that all circumstances are without inheritable existence or do not exist. The teaching is based on the fact that:

- Anything that is contaminated is suffering.
- No permanency of substance.
- All phenomenon are devoid of self and are empty.
- True peace is Nirvana.

The 5 Skandhas

The five skandhas in Buddhism are referred to as Sanskrit, Pali, Bengali, and Sinhala. Each stands for the form or material image, the sensation or feeling got from the form, perceptions, mental activity, and consciousness, respectively.

The 5 Precepts of Buddhism

The teachings are rules that each individual who is truly practicing Buddhism has to live by every day. It is not a commandment, but the followers of the religion are to keep these rules which they should guard against intelligently, and they are:

1. **Avoid Killing:** This teaching directs every individual to be peaceful, to shun violence and to take the life of another person or living beings, and also to respect life. Hence protecting life is connected to these precepts. To go deeper into the rules or teaching, the Buddhist suggests such an individual to become a vegetarian and never to support or participate in the killing of another.

2. **Avoid Stealing:** The rule on refraining from stealing teaches non-conversion of other people's property, which does not belong to

you. It also teaches to avoid wasting the time of other people by turning it to something else. For example, respect your employer's time he gives you as working hours and don't waste it. It teaches generosity and compassion.

3. **Avoid Sexual Misconduct:** This teaching talks about avoiding all forms of sexual immorality, especially adultery and rape, which often leads to mental abuse and physical injury.

4. **Do not lie:** This is a warning not to lie and always tell the truth. No exaggeration, no adding to what is already the truth, and nothing like half-truth will stand as the truth.

5. **Avoid Drugs and Alcohol:** This rule, if broken, has dishonored every other rule. Buddhism is a meditating religion, and if the mind becomes intoxicated, it will not be able to achieve the aims and objectives of Buddhism. Drugs and alcohol should be avoided at all costs because they are considered harmful to health.

Perfections of Buddhism

There are 10 perfections in the tradition of the Theravada, and they are: generosity known as Dana, morality known as "Sila", insight known as Panna, renunciation known as "Nekhamma", energy known as "Viriya", truthfulness known as "Sacca", patience known as "Khanti", loving-kindness known as Metta, resolution known as "Adhitthana", and equanimity known as "Upekkha".

The 6 Perfections of Mahayana Buddhism

The development of the six perfections in Mahayana Buddhism among the major Buddhist adherence was held as the standard which they ought to abide with. They are categorized as the Mahayana Sutras, which are:

1) Wisdom
2) Generosity
3) Morality
4) Vigor
5) Patience
6) Concentration

CHAPTER 5

Mindfulness Meditation

The teaching of Buddha states that in gaining understanding, all things are not permanent and not capable of giving ultimate satisfaction. Such understanding makes an individual become a Buddha, which means the "awakened one." The final goal for a Buddha is to get to that status of enlightenment. Meditation is a vital technique to get to that state. Mindfulness meditation is the psychological procedure of deliberate attempts through which an individual brings his attention to experience moments void of judgment. This is achievable through the practice of meditation and other mindfulness training. Mindfulness training is a major and essential aspect of Buddhism traditions; the techniques involved in mindfulness meditation are wide. Mindfulness meditation takes an individual to the past, present, and future.

Benefits of Mindfulness

Mindfulness is very good when we are able to develop a habit of it through Buddhism practice. Some benefits are as follows:

- **Having a healthier mind:** Mindfulness enables an individual to have a healthier mind that is detached from depression and all the worries and difficulties associated with an unhealthy mind.
- **Healthy body:** It enables an individual to develop a healthy body that can stand emotional pain and stress, both physical and spiritual. It also helps in the development of psychic energy, which leads to a better immune system.
- **Resilient Mind:** This enables a person to have a very strong mind that can withstand hardship. It is based on being content, having a deeper understanding about suffering, and that there is a cause for it, which will be brought to an end according to the Buddhist way. The individual has contentment when he gains a deeper awakening of himself.
- **Stable Mind:** Mindfulness will help an individual to have a better and more stable mind, unlike a fearfully made mindset. It helps

to develop better consciousness and openness to experience.

- **Improved relationship and social life:** With the development of great compassion for friends, neighbors, and strangers, mindfulness enables a person to become a Buddhist practitioner. One who understands the art of showing kindness and relating to people.
- **Improved level of awareness:** Mindfulness helps the development of self-awareness and awakening the deep insight that was hitherto unknown to the individual. The learning process exposes him to a great self-experience.
- **Greater Insight:** Mindfulness helps one discover the individual self in relation to internal peace and happiness, which has eluded many people in the world today; the path to happiness is mindfulness.

Training the Mind

In the Buddhist tradition, mind training is usually carried out based on a set of formulated processes recorded in the Tibet, which is 12th-century literature. It involves the purifying and refining of an individual's motivations, behavior, or attitude.

Freeing your Mind

The teaching of Buddhism is all-round based on mindfulness as the basics to develop the mind. It is a way of life that focuses on nurturing a mind to become very healthy. The Buddhist concept has been applied to develop the mind as a means of therapeutic practice. Freeing your mind can help you to get a better understanding, just like the case of Buddha. By meditating and silently allowing the thoughts to pass by, getting inner meaning is to focus on self even while you are in the midst of the vagaries of life. You are practicing self-reflection and detachment of your thoughts from what goes on around you.

Classic Mindfulness Meditation Step-By-Step

Mantras are sounds or words replicated to aid the concentration of the mind during meditation. This is believed by Buddhists to aid the spiritual and physical mindfulness during the meditation process. The mantra is now viewed in modern times as the "intention." It has now been further split into two forms which are "man" meaning the "mind" and "tra" which means "vehicle." Therefore, the mantra is a spiritual instrument of sound or vibration that you can utilize to enter into a deep state of meditation.

The quality of mindfulness meditation can be achieved by a simple exercise in a step-by-step process, which was adopted over 2,600 years ago by Buddha viz-a-viz:

- **Breath Awareness:** Pay attention to your breath, concentrate on the sensation of the breaths in your nostrils all through the expansion and contraction in your chest or belly. Avoid controlling your breath, but only observe it and calm naturally. It can be difficult at first but do your best.
- **Count Your Breaths:** The in and out breaths should be counted, that is, your inhaling and exhaling to about ten times. Don't get distracted, but if you do, repeat the process. It's not a competition; it's about your efforts.
- **Acknowledge Your Feelings and Sensations but Do Not Judge:** the focus is concentrating on the breath during meditation. It is possible you'll get body sensations or thoughts or feelings, but don't lose focus.

Repeat the process until your meditation sessions end.

Different Buddhist Rituals

There are varying practices and rituals in Buddhism that enable an individual's journey into great enlightenment. These rituals were inspired by already established religions in parts of Asia, especially India, Japan, China, Tibet, etc. In summary, some rituals and practices in Buddhism are:

- Meditation which dwells on concentration and mindfulness.
- Mantras, which is based on sacred sound or phrases.
- Mudras, which is the teaching on symbolic hand gestures.
- The Prayer Wheels, which are the recitation.
- The Monasticism.
- The pilgrimage to sacred locations.
- The veneration or referencing of Deities and Buddhas.

CHAPTER 6

Japanese Buddhism

Buddhism was introduced in Japan in 552 CE; this was when the official introduction was made. Since its introduction in Japan, the impact of Buddhism has led to the development of Japanese culture and society. This has become a great history of Buddhism. In modern day Japan, the famous schools of Buddhism are the Nichiren, Shingon, Zen and Pure Land. About 34% of Japanese people have been practicing Buddhism since 2008 and the number has been increasing since then. About 60% of the people of Japan already have Buddhist shrines in their various homes.

Buddhism In This Era

The study of Buddhism in the modern era has been in demand. If it has to be practiced and gain wider experience, it must be expanded to the scope of evangelism. This can be done using the modern-day media to spread the message, doctrines, and benefits of participating in Buddhism. Buddhism will go a long way to impact greatly on the society in terms of quality of the individuals that we will have in the world, which is going to be a whole new generation of people. There is a need to shift from conservatism that dwells on ritual and prayer only to a much more universal inclusion. The 21st century has also brought in technology advancement. With the information and communication age impacting greatly on the society, Buddhism needs to be reviewed and ways of fashioning out means of communicating to people all around the world.

Creating an environment where Buddhism will fit into the challenges of the 21st century created by the information and internet era is what should be considered by the Buddhist. It's not about preserving the culture and tradition of Buddhism. But it's about posterity, how will Buddhism be transmitted to the next generation? What is the right education for our teaming generation? How are we going to pass the tradition to the modern era? Western education may take over the minds of our next generation without the input of Buddhism. All the history and secret traditions of mindfulness will be gone with history if Buddhism is not revisited with new innovations to the education of Buddhism to the next generation. The new and next-generation really needs enlightenment in an era that is filled with materialism and so much attachment. The best time to take action on Buddhism ideals to be inculcated is now.

Transmission of Buddhism from one generation to another in history has started from one enlightened person the (Buddha) who passed it down through oral teachings. These teachings were repeated by students and disciples until someone decided to put it down in writing. From writing, we have oral tradition and scriptures. So what's going to be the next documentation and teaching in the modern era of the great internet and information age? Certainly, Buddhism needs to upgrade to match with the trend.

Buddha's enlightened words have been written on palms, stones, leaves, walls etc. Just to keep and teach them. It has been translated in different languages and distributed in Asia and other continents for those who would care to listen. People in the modern era have received information via emails and videos. People easily have access to videos and websites that distribute information. Buddhism should not be exempted from exploiting these processes to educate. With schools all over the world now embracing online courses and trainings, the challenge is on Buddhism schools to start something that will make them accessible online. Many of the Buddhism schools would gain more membership all over the world if they are ready to accommodate more converts now and in the future. This can be done by expanding the scope of the knowledge of gaining enlightenment to help the world in solving the problems caused by materialism, attachment, and lack of mindfulness, which are the major causes of several problems in the world.

Creating a Meditation Space in Your Home

To create a space in your room for meditation, there are no specific rules. However, there are standards to follow which will help you in carrying out a good meditation, and they are:

- Pick a space that you feel good in.
- Make your meditation room clean.
- Make the room comfortable.
- Provide adequate lighting.
- Make it natural.
- Make it private and personalized.
- Make it have a decent fragrance.
- Let it be part of you.

5 Steps to Start Buddhist Meditation

Meditation is basically based on mindfulness. The best way to do it is to take it simply; follow these steps and tips:

1) Get a good spot for your meditation.

2) Choose a comfortable position.

3) Free your mind.

4) Sit and observe.

5) Practice and end your meditation.

How to Practice Buddhism

If you want to live a peaceful, happy, and mindful life, you can start practicing Buddhism. If you want to discover yourself through a great awakening and want to be more enlightened in the matters of life and beyond, definitely Buddhism can lead you in the right path to achieving them. Unlike other religions that teach about deities and spiritual laws, Buddhism dwells more on personal transformation and essence. There are different sects of Buddhism, irrespective of this. They have foundational understanding that all the Buddhist sects share which arises from a basic teaching and foundational processes that relate to all the traditional practices.

Some of these fundamental basics are suffering, kindness and openness. To start practicing Buddhism, here are some tips:

To start with, there are four vows which are very great Bodhisattva and which you must keep, viz-a-viz:

- **Working to end the suffering of others:** The teaching of the four noble truths can help in this regard. It reminds us that suffering can come to an end. There is a cause and there is a path to the end of that cause. It teaches the cycle of life which is birth, death, and rebirth, hence working towards helping others.
- **Be a disciple of the Eightfold Path:** Emphasizing on the eightfold path and following the teaching is what makes suffering no longer exist—the end of suffering. All the lessons as to speech, action, livelihood, effort meditation, concentration, thought, understanding, mindfulness, etc., and the five precepts, should be practiced.
- **Avoid Desires and Needs:** Remove your desires from wealth, don't pick interest in materialism.

Craving pleasure for these goes against Buddhism.
- **Continuous Learning:** Learn the Dharma and suffering. Learning is a lifelong journey which should not be limited; it will enable you to widen your enlightenment.
- **Practice Buddhism:** Especially the basics of the Buddhist lifestyle, and understanding the rules behind each teaching, especially that of karma.
- **Meditation:** Practice your meditation on a daily basis to increase your mindfulness. The more you practice, the more enlightened you will become. These are the paths to follow to start practicing your Buddhism. Explore the tradition that has impacted on millions of people around the world. It may take you some time but definitely, it is going to greatly help you become awakened or enlightened.

Practicing Mindfulness Meditation for Stress and Anxiety Relief

The practice of mindfulness meditation for stress and anxiety relief can be done based on focusing your attention on something which starts from yourself—the mindfulness to get stress relief. This process enables you to pay more attention to objects of sound, and the focal point is that these objects come from within. Doing a focus meditation is possible, and you don't need an instructor. However, it should be a personal experience in a quiet environment. A focus meditation is achievable when you fix your mindfulness on the present without wandering off. The elements involved are the sound, the meditation, the breath. Take your mind off the stress you are going through and be more interested in the self breath and practice. For stress relief, more focused meditation is ideal. This is because your attention is taken away from what is causing the stress and put into utilization by taking your mind off the past and on the present.

The most important thing to note is that this meditation can be practiced at home or anywhere that is quiet. Your office may be good, but if it is noisy, it's not a conducive environment. The idea is to relieve yourself of the stress.

Your meditation can start with 5-minute sessions, and you can later develop it by working your way up until it becomes comfortable. You play with it and exercise with it as well. The idea is to start getting used to it as quickly as possible since stress is often caused by working conditions that we are subjected to in our offices. You have to learn to enjoy the moment of meditation.

- Focus on your breath because it is the entry point to any form of meditation and will help you remain focused.
- Getting into a comfortable position will enable you to relieve stress. Sitting upright can be good, or you can choose the one that best suits you, using a chair or sitting on the ground, whichever is comfortable. Remember, the idea is to relieve stress. Be in a relaxed mode, and make sure you don't fall asleep. Choose any of the meditation positions earlier described in this book.
- Target your attention on yourself: being mindfully present at the moment is important, so pay attention to the sensations you experience as you breathe in and out of your body.
- Reduce your inner voice: don't listen to the inner voice that tends to analyze the stressful situation you have been through. Meditate on the present and the future, turn your mind to the sensation it provides. The goal is to keep a quiet mind void of interaction with stress.
- Avoid thinking about Failure: nobody is perfect; don't let failures begin to run in your mind. It's understandable that a person may be going through difficulty, but when you start

your meditation, avoid the temptation of thinking about your failures. The process is to help you overcome it and not stressing yourself even more with thoughts of failure.

Other factors that will help your meditation, as stated earlier, are timing, shorter sessions of meditation to relieve stress, and meditation practice. By the time you start getting the best of the practice, you will notice a stress relief, having more self-awareness and improved memory. The more you practice, the better your chances of getting the right results.

Buddhism for Children

Buddhism was the exclusive preserve of the adult from the beginning. The teachings were for mature minds, and the demands of the commitments could only be carried out by adults. But as the enlightenment began to spread, the teachings, especially of Dharma, were taught to children. Teachings based on kindness, good deeds, respect, etc. were taught to children so that they would connect to their lives. Most children in the early Indian societies were confined to their homes and doing house core activities before the gradual dharma teachings were taught to them.

The Buddha himself was married and before leaving his royal palace, he had a little son.

Western authors have criticized Buddha for leaving his son Rahula Pali behind to go after seeking enlightenment. But Buddhist authors have said it was justifiable because he went out in pursuit of a higher course, which is enlightenment.

Pali Rahula, Buddha's son, however, later became a disciple of his father at age seven. Buddha taught his son the seeds of his teachings and the truthfulness which he saw in them. Teachings like, in your quest to seek the truth about life, you will have to be truthful to yourself. Some teachings he also gave his son included, using his actions as a mirror before doing anything. That actions should be supported with the fact that the end product will be good and not bad. But if the action is bad and harmful, there was no need to embark on doing such actions. After doing good actions, he still has to question his conscience if what he did actually brought well-being to those affected. That action should always be accompanied by a pleasant result—consequence. It should be well thought out and skillfully made in order to achieve the good result. He also taught his young son that if actions brought good results, then it is deserving to stay mentally informed and refreshed, and be joyful.

Having trainings both in the day and in the night in skillful mental development should be of good quality.

The children in our era can also be led in this path of education to really get deeper into the realities of life, to help in their development in life. Buddha continued to teach his son the realities of taking responsibilities for his own actions, and never to repeat the same mistakes twice. He taught him the path of the noble truths.

The teaching of Buddhism for children is seen to be more successful with societies that are used to a higher level of tradition and spirituality. Societies such as some parts of Asia where the religion of Buddhism seems to have taken root and children are also taught on the tenets of Buddhism.

However, there are challenges in the teaching of Buddhism in the modern era. Especially in the information age where the internet and mobile gadgets, especially mobile phones, pads, and computers, are now taking over the world in terms of education, business, and daily life. There is no day a young person is not surfing the internet.

How can Buddhists successfully help this generation of young people to practice the faith?

Schools can set up volunteer centers where we can start with teachers who are able to impart the knowledge. Then students who can participate in gaining enlightenment can begin to enroll in the school. The authorities will have to create an enabling environment for the successful take off of such noble activity. Seminars, articles, and more awareness have to be created to enable this project to expand and reach other parts of the world.

Most youths who would have trained their minds in the paths of Buddhism have been lured into crime. They have constituted public nuisances and developed habits that are unfit or unethical in the society. If only Buddhism would be exposed to these youths to help develop their minds and take them away from drugs, away from the streets and make them venture into the noble life of Buddhism, the world would become a better place.

CHAPTER 7

CONCLUSION

You have had the opportunity to access a great revelation needed for an individual's transformation, as well as impactful teaching that will transform the lives of many people. The era we are now is the stress era because we are exposed to working conditions that take our time. The office, academic activities in school, the internet and media, computers, laptops, mobile phones and devices are taking more energy out of our bodies. We need to get refreshed naturally to enable the recycling of energy or replacement of lost energy through the Buddhism practice of mindfulness meditation.

We now understand that anxiety and stress are some of the enemies of human beings and there will always be a need to end them. The inevitability of our beginning and ending, especially the teaching on the causation of suffering, the fact about life, the cessation of suffering and the path that leads to its cessation, are well understood. We have to grasp the enlightenment that is unknown to many people in the world today. We get the enlightenment by being exposed to the reality of why Buddhism came into existence. How it all began, and how it has transformed the lives of over four hundred million people around the world. What, hitherto, was knowledge that we knew nothing about, has been revealed through this book. Mere knowledge and information without implementation will be useless if we want to get the reality of practicing Buddhism. Until we start, we will not get results by merely reading for the sake of knowledge without implementing it.

Everything in life has karma, and practicing the Dharma will help us to avoid negative karma that will bring unpalatable consequences, as the teaching implies. We have understood why people suffer, and we know how to mitigate or bring the suffering phenomena to a cessation through the practice of Buddhism. The knowledge we have gained is huge, and I am sure several people who have access to this book will be more than happy to start practicing what is in the contents.

True happiness and transformation via set down practicable principles and precepts are what characterize Buddhism. It is not about the promotion of Buddhism. Rather, it is about the benefits you stand to gain when you get enlightenment through the traditions and teachings of Buddhism. You not only become the Buddha yourself, but you will also be able to impact positively on the lives of people. You will do this by taking them through a path that will lead them to the truth of a hidden knowledge. This will help them to develop mentally and spiritually.

Imagine if we have many more Buddhists in the society, how much better our world would be. Take a look at societies like Japan that have exploited Buddhism to develop great minds who are thinking very effectively. The Japanese lifestyle of Buddhism has even helped the country to gain more advancement than other countries that don't have the Buddhist approach to life. The time to get awakened is now. With your ability to read and digest the contents of this book, and the zeal to see to it that you start practicing it, you will absolutely become transformed and enlightened forever. Congratulations on choosing the path to your great awakening! Good luck!

www.ingramcontent.com/pod-product-compliance
Lightning Source LLC
Chambersburg PA
CBHW070908080526
44589CB00013B/1224